Terry Virgo has spent a lifetim
and drawing out their significance for today, and it snows. in God's
Treasured Possession he opens up the life of Moses, the greatest
of Old Testament figures, and his exposition is full of insight,
application and pastoral wisdom.
Andrew Wilson, Teaching Pastor, King's Church London

As theologically solid as the best commentaries and as practical
and uplifting as the best devotionals, these bite-sized reflections on
the life of Moses challenge and inspire in equal measure.
Sam Hailes, editor of Premier Christianity *magazine and elder at
Christ Central Church in Penge and Crystal Palace*

I love Terry's reminder that beginning with Moses, as Jesus told
the travellers to Emmaus, all that had been revealed in scripture
was about him. All of it – written for our sake. Thus he whets
the appetite to dig in. What one finds is a feast, particularly for
Christian parents seeking to bequeath this treasured possession
of faith to their children. As such a parent, this book gave me hope
to keep praying for my children as they wrestle with choosing
between all that this world promises over the harder to grasp
treasure that I want them to take hold of. This hope is fed as I read a
moving portrait of the young man Moses coming into the fullness
of his inheritance as part of God's treasured possession.
Esther Prior, Vicar, St John's Egham

I am happy to recommend this book which could only have
been written by a veteran pastor with a deep understanding of

the human heart. In chapter after chapter Terry Virgo explains the spiritual dynamics in each event in the life of Moses, gives insight into appropriate New Testament parallels and fulfillments and then provides practical wisdom that I think will be both challenging and helpful to every Christian who seeks a deeper personal relationship with God himself.

Wayne Grudem, Distinguished Research Professor of Theology and Biblical studies, Phoenix Seminary, USA

For years many have benefited from listening to Terry Virgo preach on the life of Moses. Now Terry has given a gift to us all; he has written down a lifetime of his insights and reflections on this servant of God which we can all benefit from. This wonderful book will encourage you, challenge you and draw you closer to God. You cannot fail to benefit from it as you read it, treasure it and take its message to heart.

David Stroud, Senior Leader of Christ Church London and Co-founder of Everything Conference

Reading this book by Terry Virgo will make you feel as if you are tasting honey. It flows from the clear mind and warm heart of one of God's most admired servants. If this is your first book of Terry's to read, you will soon see why this is so. Get prepared to be both challenged and encouraged from start to finish.

Dr RT Kendall, former Minister of Westminster Chapel, London

No one has captivated me like Moses. He was one of the few that ultimately did not want leadership because he really did understand what it would cost him. Nor was his fulfilment in his mission – it was in God. The story of leading the children of Israel out of Egypt is rich for us today. Now, add to that Terry Virgo's insights to him and you have an incredible book that is hard to put down. I love the format of the book, which tells the stories in an engaging way and then forces you to ask questions about what it means for us. No one has impacted me more than Terry Virgo. He is a rare leader. Everyone will get something out of this book.

Bob Roberts, Founder of Northwood Church and Glocalnet, Keller, Texas, and author of several books

With a wealth of wisdom and rich biblical knowledge Terry Virgo brings fresh insights into well-known stories in a way that equips leaders and encourages all believers. This is God's word handled in a life giving way.

Tope Koleoso, Pastor of Jubilee Church, London

Terry Virgo opens the book of Exodus and helps us to see how the stories it tells were "written for us". Whilst highly accessible and easy to read, this book is not a simplistic devotional. It combines deep exegetical insights with biblical theological interpretation that takes us from Moses to Christ and then draws lessons for our own Christian lives and service. Terry draws engagingly on many experiences from his own ministry to help us make personal applications. All Christians will be encouraged by this book to rejoice afresh in the astonishing grace of God that has set them free from slavery to sin. Church leaders will be especially encouraged to face challenges, disappointments and failures with renewed confidence in God's call and the powerful presence of the Holy Spirit.

John Stevens, National Director of FIEC

Terry Virgo is one of my spiritual heroes – someone who has greatly enriched the lives of many, including my own. This book on the life of Moses is classic Terry; an amazingly comprehensive yet skilfully concise portrayal, filled with clear biblical insights, personal illustrations and practical application. Read and be blessed.

Dave Smith, pastor of Kingsgate Church and author of several books

GOD'S TREASURED POSSESSION

GOD'S TREASURED POSSESSION

Walk in the footsteps of Moses

Terry Virgo

INTER-VARSITY PRESS
36 Causton Street, London SW1P 4ST, England
Email: ivp@ivpbooks.com
Website: www.ivpbooks.com
© Terry Virgo 2021

Terry Virgo has asserted his right under the Copyright, Designs and Patents Act, 1988, to be identified as Author of this work.

Unless otherwise indicated, Scripture quotations are taken from the HOLY BIBLE, NEW INTERNATIONAL VERSION. Copyright © 1973, 1978, 1984 by International Bible Society. Used by permission of Hodder & Stoughton Publishers, a member of the Hachette UK Group. All rights reserved. 'niv' is a registered trademark of International Bible Society. UK trademark number 1448790.

Scripture quotations marked esv are from the ESV Bible (The Holy Bible, English Standard Version), copyright © 2001 by Crossway, a publishing ministry of Good News Publishers. Used by permission. All rights reserved.

Scripture quotations marked nkjv are taken from the New King James Version. Copyright © 1982 by Thomas Nelson, Inc. Used by permission. All rights reserved.

First published 2021

British Library Cataloguing-in-Publication Data
A catalogue record for this book is available from the British Library.

ISBN: 978-1-78974-297-8
eBook ISBN 978-1-78974-302-9
1 3 5 7 9 10 8 6 4 2

Set in Minion Pro 10.25/13.75pt
Typeset in Great Britain by The Book Guild Ltd, Leicester
Printed and bound by CPI Group (UK) Ltd, Croydon CR0 4YY

Produced on paper from sustainable forests

Inter-Varsity Press publishes Christian books that are true to the Bible and that communicate the gospel, develop discipleship and strengthen the church for its mission in the world.

IVP originated within the Inter-Varsity Fellowship, now the Universities and Colleges Christian Fellowship, a student movement connecting Christian Unions in universities and colleges throughout Great Britain, and a member movement of the International Fellowship of Evangelical Students. Website: www.uccf.org.uk. That historic association is maintained, and all senior IVP staff and committee members subscribe to the UCCF Basis of Faith.

I dedicate this book to members past and present of a church I served for many years, known from time to time as Brighton and Hove Christian Fellowship, Clarendon Church, Church of Christ the King and now Emmanuel. Many of us enjoyed a journey together from our tiny beginnings, facing many challenges and experiencing God's wonderful sufficiency.

And let me express my gratitude especially to one of its outstanding members, Janis Peters, who served as my PA for 24 years and gladly stepped up again to type this manuscript for me.

Contents

Contents

Note to the reader

As I present this book to you, I ask myself how have I benefitted from writing it? As I have lived with the story, I have found fresh courage in the face of perplexity and growing strength in refusing to yield to setbacks. I believe I have grown in my confidence in a covenant-keeping God and been amazed at His patience and kindness towards His wayward people.

His delight in Israel as His treasured possession defies our understanding. They continually failed Him with gross disloyalty, but He insisted on showing them covenant love and consistent kindness.

What also becomes obvious is that their ultimate success depended on a faithful mediator. Moses, as an intercessor, provided an extraordinary model of faithfulness and devotion. His determination to complete his task, see God glorified and stay true to God's recalcitrant people is a stunning and stimulating example to all who are called to shepherd God's people. But he especially reminds us of another magnificent mediator who stands before God incessantly on our behalf (Heb. 7:25).

But why did Paul write to an essentially Gentile church in Corinth reminding them of this tale of a Hebrew nation's journey? He wanted them to comprehend that Israel's story was actually their family story. Paul wrote to these Gentiles, "*our fathers* were all under the cloud and all passed through the sea. They were all baptised into Moses in the cloud and in the sea" (1 Cor. 10:1-2 my italics). Now that the Corinthians were in Christ, these Hebrews had become *their forefathers*. Ours too! (Gal. 3:29).

Note to the reader

Every lesson they learned has something to teach us about God's wonderful character. He has chosen to make himself known through dramatic stories rather than lists of divine attributes. You will find yourself in these chapters and I pray that you will find wisdom and strength for your journey into the inheritance God has planned for you.

1

A story written for us

On the Road to Emmaus. Luke 24:13–27

The road seemed endless. They had left Jerusalem over an hour ago, just two figures in the stream of pilgrims leaving Jerusalem after the Passover Feast. Many were chattering and exclaiming as they talked about the events of the last few days, but Cleopas and his companion were subdued, their hearts heavier than their feet. The crowds thinned out as they continued westward, the sun beginning to sink on the horizon.

Preoccupied with their thoughts, the disciples hadn't talked much, but now they began to discuss in low voices the events of the past few days. Their hopes and dreams were shattered and as they trudged along the familiar route, everything seemed grey and purposeless.

A slight footfall behind them made Cleopas turn his head to see a figure coming alongside them.

The stranger greeted them and fell into step.

'What are you two discussing so intently?' he asked.

They stopped walking and sighed.

'You must be a visitor!' remarked Cleopas. 'Don't you know what has been going on?'

'What things?'

'About Jesus of Nazareth', they replied in unison, and went on to describe how this amazing man, whom they had hoped would be the Messiah, had been crucified. Yet some women had been to the tomb where he was buried and the body had gone!

'How foolish you are!' exclaimed the stranger. 'Don't you know that the prophets spoke about these things?'

Then followed the most enthralling hour of their lives as, beginning with Moses, he unfolded the story of the Jewish nation, and showed them how it all pointed to the coming Christ. He highlighted the centre of the plot, the fact that underneath all the revelation of prophets, kings, sacrifices and promised inheritance was one awesome figure. The story had climaxed in a dramatic and necessary sacrifice – yet it did not end in death, but resurrection and life!

Having thrilled their hearts with the biblical narrative, Jesus seemed as if he was to leave them, but they prevailed upon him to linger. It was only as he broke bread that their eyes were opened to his true identity. His purpose as they walked on the road was not simply to show them a spectacular miracle and capture their interest. His primary purpose was that they understood the story.

Story not systematic theology

We all enjoy a good story. We like getting caught up in the plot, meeting the characters, sharing their experiences and being drawn into the twists and turns of the narrative. The Bible is full not of what we have come to call systematic theology, with lists of attributes of God, but of extraordinary characters and events. We teach them to our children and fight for their veracity – but, of course, the stories of the Bible provide so much more than entertainment.

Writing to the church in Corinth, Paul explained, 'These things

2

happened to them as examples and were written down as warnings for us, on whom the culmination of the ages has come.' (1 Cor. 10:11). Ancient events not only 'happened', they are not only solid history that took place at a certain time and place to real flesh and blood people. They were recorded with a distinct purpose, namely to instruct us.

Yet we live in a different age, you might protest. Yes, what Paul called 'the ends of the ages'. As catastrophes of apocalyptic proportion seem to be taking place around the globe, massive forest fires, climate change, a global pandemic, droughts, floods and famine (to name just a few of the 'natural' disasters), time is manifestly rushing on and, maybe, running out. Yet our unchanging God has provided instruction for us on our journey.

Through these days of rapid change, we desperately need a map and compass.

A lot of people find it easier to learn about God through reading stories rather than studying concepts and wrestling with ideas. We can identify with people, their victories, difficulties and defeats. We are told to 'to imitate those who through faith and patience inherit what has been promised' (Heb. 6:12). So, having models to imitate is helpful, but if we are to imitate successfully, we need to study their experience carefully.

Exodus is often presented as a book about liberation from slavery. This is how Hollywood depicts it through a twenty-first century perspective. However, if that was all it were, it would end with the parting of the Red Sea, the escape of the Israelites and the destruction of the Egyptian army.

Freedom accomplished!

Although the story reaches a great climax at the famous Red Sea crossing, the plot continues to a breathtaking encounter at Sinai, the giving of the Law and the construction of the tabernacle, then onward to the Promised Land. Exodus is far more than a tale of liberation.

The birth of a nation

Exodus is the story of how God gave birth to a nation, the creation of Israel. Although the twelve tribes had multiplied through spectacular growth in Egypt, they did not become a nation until Yahweh created them as such through the exodus. Their identity as the people of God, a people belonging to God as His possession, is rooted in their experience of redemption and rescue. No other god had done such for any other people. They were uniquely his, and he uniquely theirs.

Paul invites us to be instructed by Israel's journey from slavery to inheritance, from being helpless captives of a powerful and overbearing master to taking a demanding journey to a promised land, which God would freely give them if they would follow faithfully. All kinds of pitfalls, snares and dangers awaited them, but they would also come to experience God's extraordinary patience, covenant love and ability to provide. Ultimately, they were to emerge as 'a great nation, a wise and understanding people' (Deut. 4:6), but their greatness differed from the wealth or military might that constituted other great nations. Their unique claim was an unparalleled boast, 'What other nation is so great as to have their gods near them the way the Lord our God is near us whenever we pray to him?' (Deut. 4:7)[1].

In our story, the role of leadership will become evident. Moses emerged as a colossus of massive significance: 'They were baptised into Moses in the cloud and in the sea' (1 Cor. 10:2). He was their shepherd and their prophet, his role cannot be overstated. Yet they were led by the cloud that God himself provided, together with manna and water from the rock. All these things are seen by Paul as markers and guides for us in our journey from our initial slavery to the inheritance God has placed before us.

Let me encourage you then to see each chapter in this little book not merely as a fascinating story, but a warning, an encouragement, a signpost on your journey that you might arrive strengthened and fortified as you observe His ways and His faithfulness with His people. These things were written down for our instruction. Let us read and be instructed.

2

By faith Moses refused

An Origin Story. Exodus 2:1–10

What a time to be born! Not only were his parents slaves, but the latest draconian law established that all the Israelite baby boys should be slaughtered. Welcome to a world of horrendous peril. We don't get to choose where we will be born, but if a choice could be made, few of us would select this.

Yet Moses also enjoyed an extraordinary privilege. He was born into the home of believing parents – not simply religious parents, but the kind of believers who find themselves mentioned in the classic Hebrews chapter 11, which celebrates great heroes of faith. This was privilege indeed!

Today some Christians express regret at having been raised in a believing family, feeling they lack a dynamic black and white conversion testimony with the drama of being saved and rescued from a debauched life. "I was raised in a Christian home" is the last thing we want to own up to. However, Moses' parents were far from nominal in their faith, which led them to take a distinctly dangerous decision. Their faith overcame fear and they refused the king's edict. Moses lived, saved by their active, living faith.

And then a completely unforeseen development.

Having been concealed, a new risky step.

Launched in a basket on the shallows of the Nile and discovered by no less than Pharaoh's daughter who, moved with compassion, rescued him and even responded to his sister's appeal that one of the Hebrew slave women look after him.

Now, back with his parents, he could learn what had sustained and inspired them through their years of slavery. They had an amazing sense of destiny and hope. Moses must have come to understand who the slave community really were, namely a nation whose ultimate earthly father, Abraham, lived with a phenomenal promise from God of worldwide significance. Asked if he could count the stars, Abraham was promised that so many would his descendants be and that, ultimately, through his descendants, all the families of the earth were to be blessed.

A stunning vision of global proportions.

Egypt university

The slave community carried the hope of the world. Moses' parents must have fascinated and captivated him with this glorious dream, but soon it would be severely tested. He must return to Pharaoh's palace to be instructed in all of Egypt's wisdom. Egyptology continues to fascinate students centuries later. Ancient Egyptians were an extraordinary people who enjoyed breathtaking military success, and educational, architectural and medical breakthroughs of remarkable proportions.

In contrast to his parents' dreams, their progress was tangible, in your face and demonstrable. Not the mystical, unseen and spiritual hope that Moses' parents clung to. Two contrasting worlds fought for his allegiance: similar to the experience of young Christians today, raised by believing parents but suddenly away from home, face to face with a very contrasting world view presented to them at university. Every day, whatever age we are, we are confronted by the choice to put our faith in the world around us, or what the Bible tells us is true.[2] Egypt's power and accomplishments were so great, so impressive. Our modern secular world with all its arguments can be so persuasive. Which to trust? Which to pursue?

Moses was instructed in all the wisdom of Egypt through the best teachers money could buy. We are told he became "mighty in word and deeds" (Acts 7:22 KJV). Josephus, the Jewish historian, records that he led an Egyptian army against the Ethiopians and won a great victory at Memphis.[3] He seems to have left his past behind him and become an impressive and no doubt privileged Egyptian prince.

Nevertheless, an internal conflict continued. He could not escape the vision passed on to him by his parents. In spite of his position of security, pleasure, multiplied resources and all that a young man might dream of, Moses, when he reached maturity, made a staggering choice. We read these remarkable words, "By faith Moses refused…" (Heb. 11:24). Rather a different position to the so-called 'prosperity gospel' which encourages us that by faith we can accumulate. His was a far more radical faith stance. It led to his ability to see through what was on offer in Egypt and become stirred and fascinated by God's plan invested in Israel.

Although they appeared weak, vulnerable and insignificant slaves, he truly believed that they held world history in their midst. Moses will of course always be associated with the law, but it's vital to understand that Moses' decision was based on faith. Faith was the ultimate key, as was demonstrated in his forefather Abraham.

Moses was not forced into this decision by his godly parents. He made the choice freely when he had reached a mature age. No law required him to do it. Faith led him to his refusal. This is such

8

a key to living the life God wants from His people. Though He is God and it is so appropriate that He should be obeyed, He looks for an obedience based on faith, not reluctance.

Obedience motivated by faith

Paul regarded his apostolic ministry as calling 'all the Gentiles to the obedience that comes from faith' (Rom. 1:5 NIV). God wants us to obey Him because we genuinely trust him.

The plague that has ruined the human race is not rooted in selfishness, as some might suggest, but unbelief. Satan challenged Adam and Eve that they should not believe God. God was holding out on them, He could not be trusted. If they ate what Satan offered, they could be as gods, making their own choices about good and evil (Gen. 3:15).

Why would anyone take God at His word?

God must have been delighted with Moses' choice. By faith he refused the easy path. No parents were breathing down his neck and no law was demanding 'you shall not', but he was motivated by pure trust in God's promise, His love and His wisdom. The nation of Israel looked far from impressive. Utterly powerless, poor and enslaved, while Egypt ruled the world and was able to demonstrate phenomenal success. Naked faith in what God had promised evidently captivated Moses. No longer a child and far from parental control, he made his courageous choice.

For myself, I remember coming out of a period of serious teenage backsliding and wanting now to live a proper Christian life. Formerly I had often attended outrageous parties. Now, trying to live as a Christian, I found myself invited again, but refusing to take part. As I understood it, I was still struggling with the

9

temptation and was not making my choice by faith. I refused to attend because Christians were not allowed to attend such parties.

Of course, this undermined my evangelistic endeavours. I could invite my friends to become Christians, then they would not be allowed to go to these parties either! Such an unattractive invitation. Later, I came to see more clearly the wonder of my Christian life and was able to refuse by faith, counting it greater riches to be associated with the despised people of God and the wonders of knowing Christ.

By faith Moses refused it all, because he genuinely believed God.

God wants our trust, not our reluctant obedience. By faith Abraham left the security of the Ur of the Chaldeans and now Moses, by faith, chose to believe God not in a casual acknowledgement, but in a life-changing step of absolute dependence on His word. He began an adventure rooted in God's faithfulness.

The question arises, will you trust Him enough to obey and make choices that glorify Him and make it clear where your hope lies, and that what the world offers might look fleetingly attractive, but ultimately will prove empty?

3

Running ahead of God

Our hero gets it wrong... Exodus 2:11–25

Such good intentions, but such a blunder! He meant well but handled it so badly. Moses had made a costly inward choice not to take advantage of his cosy lifestyle in the lap of luxury, and instead fully identify with the despised slaves, but he had much to learn.

As a young, self-confident prince he took action. Seeing an Egyptian mistreating a Hebrew slave, Moses erupted from the palace and with righteous indignation killed and buried the Egyptian. With no further plan at this stage he then withdrew to the palace. The next day, seeing two Hebrews fighting, he again emerged to scold them, but to his horror they turned on him demanding to know who he thought he was. 'Who made you a ruler or judge over us? Are you going to kill us like you killed the Egyptian?' (Exod. 2:14). Devastation! His murder of the Egyptian was not as secret as he had thought, nor was his intervention appreciated, but apparently resented.

Dismayed and confused, he ran for it.

What Hebrews 11 describes as an inward, noble and costly decision looks more like reckless impetuosity and fruitless risk. No doubt he had developed a sense of his own significance as a young prince, used to taking initiatives and not particularly needing anyone's permission. Acts 7:25 tells us he supposed that his brothers understood that God was granting them deliverance through him. Yet he supposed too much!

In fact, God had neither sent nor authorized him to intervene.

He had run ahead of God, a serious mistake.

Later on in the story we see Moses fully called and commissioned by God, which will prove very different. It has been said that God has more problems with those trying to help him than he has with backsliders!

Later, when Moses had been powerfully commissioned by God and even after a breathtaking deliverance through the Red Sea, he would find that he was leading a recalcitrant people, full of their own ideas, wilfulness and outright rebellion.

God's personal authorization is fundamental to our serving him. The Good Samaritan was commended for a spontaneous act of human kindness, sacrificially outworked; but to suppose that you are God's servant, acting on his behalf, when God has not sent you smacks of presumption. I recall a fellow student telling me many years ago that he planned to go into politics, but if he did not make it there he planned to become a clergyman. He would find somewhere to speak and express himself.

Sent by God

Paul, in contrast to my friend, introduced himself as an apostle. This apostleship was not through men, nor through the agency of man, but through Jesus Christ and God the Father (Gal. 1:1), the only true credentials for serving and representing him. Jesus only did what the Father showed him and said only what the Father told him. Urged on by his own unbelieving brothers to go public in Jerusalem, he told them that they were free to go whenever they liked, but he had no such liberty, his time had not yet fully come (John 7:4–8).

Moses had a marathon before him, not a quick dash. He was God's choice, uniquely protected as a baby, but his own efforts to rush into God's service were something of a disaster. He aimed to please, and sought to serve God's cause by his own strength and enthusiasm. If anything, he was too strong for God, who chooses the weak things to shame the strong. He doesn't choose many mighty (1 Cor. 1:26). Our young and mighty hero now had a long wait until God took a completely new initiative.

I have occasionally heard it argued that the need constitutes the call. Moses had become aware of the Hebrews' distress. Surely this in itself was a call to action? Something must be done! Regarding the lost, we might argue, how will they hear without a preacher? Yet the scripture quickly replies, 'How will they preach unless they are sent?' (Rom. 10:15).

Jesus, our ultimate model and master, said that the fields were white unto harvest. Initially that sounds like we had better get on with it! However, he quickly added that we should pray to the Lord of the harvest that he might send out labourers into the harvest field. The Lord of the harvest needs to be involved. His commissioning is all-important. The task is overwhelming.

Killing the occasional Egyptian wasn't going to get the job done. The massive exodus of a nation of slaves was going to require an almighty display of God's power, not the enthusiasm of a self-motivated young prince. Heart-breaking setbacks, disappointments and discouragements awaited him. Being motivated simply by the need will never prove adequate. It will quickly evaporate when people don't want your help.

4

A new day

God speaks. Exodus 3:1–10

After long, dreary, apparently purposeless years in the wilderness, caring for a few sheep, a new day was about to dawn.

Moses had married a woman from a different nation, had children, left his past and taken on a new identity. His life as a prince and his rash intervention were long behind him. Predictable day followed predictable day.

But why was that bush burning? Why wasn't it consumed, gone up in smoke? The extraordinary blaze captured his attention. He had to investigate. Who could imagine the shock and wonder when he heard a voice addressing him by name, and not just any voice, but a presence so glorious that he dare not look? Sandals must be removed. The very ground made holy by a breathtaking presence.

'I am the God of your father...' the earthly father who made Moses' heart burn with that extraordinary dream of a destiny and global significance. And not only the God of your father, but the covenant-keeping God of Abraham, Isaac and Jacob. The God of the story you were told, the vision that once enthralled you.

We are told, 'the God of glory appeared to our father Abraham.' Now this same God was confronting Moses. The story which seemed lost and forgotten was suddenly alive and surprisingly on course. He introduced himself as the God of the story, a God who had revealed himself to individuals like Abraham, Isaac and Jacob. This is not a God in vacuum. The Bible does not reveal God as a philosophical concept, not distant and unknowable, but one who has made himself known. We get to understand Him by observing how he related to human beings. He is a God of relationship. He made and kept promises, demonstrated faithfulness, showed mercy, made friends, intervened in complex situations.

He had proved his awesome power and faithfulness to Abraham. What had seemed impossible had happened. The old man and his barren wife had produced the promised child. Faith had been tested and tried, but God demonstrated himself faithful. Not Ishmael but Isaac would inherit. Later Jacob added his contribution. The cheat wrestled with God. The one who stole his brother's birthright found that God looked after him, brought him through and transformed him to Israel, a prince with God. These patriarchs of a great nation were introduced in very human, domestic situations of tension, scheming and favouritism, with plenty of shady characters playing their part. Nevertheless, an unrelenting purpose had unfolded. A growing family was forming.

Led into Egypt by the unexpected life of Joseph, the authentic dreamer of dreams and interpreter of visions, God's people had become a burgeoning nation. Initially welcomed with huge celebrations as Joseph's kith and kin, they were now seen as a threat to the security of Egypt. Israel had multiplied and become a nation within a nation, a clear danger to Egypt's security. As such they were now under threat of extinction. Their cry had come to God. He was about to act but, as always, he looked for a human agent to fulfil His purpose.

My people

The apparently forgotten Moses was about to become one of the greatest heroes of the Bible, a colossal figure to take his place in God's plan. And yet the story took on a completely new dimension. God himself had seen the plight of the nation. He had heard their cry and he himself had come down to deliver them. For the first time in the Bible he called them 'my people' (Exod. 3:7), a title he would subsequently use repeatedly throughout the Bible.

'I have come down to deliver them,' God announced, and added, 'Come now, I will send you.' By now Moses was no longer impressed with himself. His former recklessness had gone. His self-image was as low as it could sink. Before asking who this god was, he demanded to know how he himself was to accomplish this daunting task!

The Bible repeatedly reports this kind of response when God calls someone. Gideon argued that he was the least in his father's house and that his father's house was nothing to shout about. Jeremiah complained he was far too young. Moses asked, 'Who am I?' Though unexpected, the answer he received was the one that changed everything. The issue was not who Moses was, but who was calling and commissioning him!

Although Moses was battling with his own identity in comparison to the size of the task, what completely transformed the situation was the revelation of the one who was going to accomplish this exodus with him, for him and through him. Moses had to learn that God's power provided the key. He was not being called to a task way beyond him, he was simply being called to trust and obey a god of unlimited power and supreme, dynamic resources.

I AM who I AM, I will be who I will be, a name full of

impenetrable mystery, but full of assurance and total adequacy. Uncreated, unthreatened, untainted, self-defining; God in all His sovereignty would provide the guarantee to the story's success. Moses' weakness was irrelevant. Paul would later testify, 'When I am weak, then I am strong' (2 Cor. 12:10). Moses, now drained of self-assurance and arrogant princely power, was just the man for God. Later, he would be called the meekest man on earth – just the man God was looking for!

5

What if?

Moses is set free from his past. Exodus 4.

'What if?' What a pathetic response to one of the most awesome revelations of God in the whole Bible. God's great name had been unveiled. He is the great I AM and had guaranteed His empowering presence, and all Moses could say was, 'What if they won't believe me?' Moses was in danger of missing a huge privilege. God was calling him to an amazing historic role and he was about to turn it down. Why such a negative reaction? Why not an enthusiastic thumbs up? Surely because he had a past. He had tried before to help to rescue the slaves. It had been a disaster.

When we sense that maybe God is drawing us towards a new task we often respond similarly. Why? Like Moses, many of us also have had previous experience that has not proved successful. Our self-confidence has been damaged and we don't want to risk another failure. We can't offer God a clean sheet to write our story on. It already has blots and crossings out on it.

Moses had run ahead of God, got his fingers burned, his pride crushed and his confidence undermined. Not only that, I think we can hear a hint of resentment in his reply, 'What if they won't believe me?' He had encountered them before, tried to help them before. It was because of their previous response that he had to run for it. Because of them that he'd lost everything and was now looking after a few sheep. Because of them he was no longer in the safety of a palace.

I wonder how many times it had gone around in his mind that he'd risked everything for them and they had thrown it back in his face. His brothers and sisters! Cousins! People who should never have responded like that!

Many of us have lives tainted by previous hurts and even resentments towards brothers or sisters who have let you down; maybe even sinned terribly against you, and you've been suffering because of them ever since. Maybe Christian brothers who ripped you off in business, or a Christian who seemed to be suggesting that marriage was on the cards dropped you without explanation. Maybe even Christian parents who failed you miserably, or even unspeakably. Resentment and bitterness drain our peace and wellbeing. They rob us of joy and completely dull our edge for the possibility of a new adventure. You keep your head down. You don't want to know.

We need to be set free and the way of freedom is through forgiveness and walking away free from the inner anguish that has bogged you down perhaps for years. Let me urge you to take that step into freedom. Maybe everything in you wants to argue, 'It's not fair!' By refusing to grant forgiveness you can feel that you are in control. You won't let it go. Yet the truth is that you become the one enslaved – you're the one who's trapped. Forgiveness breaks the trap and you can walk free and become open to a new future.

Send someone else!

Another crippling disease that can hold you back is simple complacency, the result of our boring and predictable life. A few sheep to be looked after day by day. This is what you do, so this is who you are. Surely after 40 years of looking after a few sheep, Moses could be tempted to think that nothing changes. His dream of seeing a nation of slaves freed to fulfil their destiny had melted like the morning dew. Expectation of a new day with him at the centre of it was long dead.

Spending all his time shepherding, he'd lost any obvious leadership skills. The one who used to be 'powerful in word and deed' complained, 'I never have been eloquent… for I am slow of speech and slow of tongue' (Exod. 4:10). How are the mighty fallen! Even when God promised to be with his mouth and teach him what to say, he pleaded that someone else should be sent (Exod. 4:13).

God had even granted him awesome signs to perform. His staff frighteningly became a snake and then returned to his familiar staff. His hand turned leprous, but happily was whole again. Yet with all this he remained stubborn, even provoking God's anger.

Finally, a way was established. Aaron, Moses' brother, would act as his spokesman, like a prophet speaking on Moses' behalf, an eloquent go-between. Moses eventually submitted to God's plan, said farewell to his father-in-law and began the trek back to Egypt, perhaps rehearsing his message to Pharaoh that Israel was God's first-born son and that if Pharaoh refused, God would kill his son, his first-born (Exod. 4:22).

Disqualified?

And then a completely unpredictable turn of events, 'The Lord met him and sought to put him to death' (Exod. 4:24). What? Put Moses to death? What's going on? There is no explanation. Was he suddenly sick to the point of death? Did they see an angel with a drawn sword? We are not told. All we know is that Moses was at death's door and *God* was responsible for this terrifying situation.

What happened next sheds the light. Without any discussion, Moses' wife Zipporah immediately circumcised their son, apparently disgusted with the operation she performed and calling her husband a bridegroom of blood. So, we are told, 'He let him alone' (Exod. 4:26). The crisis had passed. Moses survived the death threat.

What was that all about? Let me suggest an explanation. Moses was on his way to pronounce God's judgement. He would always be the man associated with God's holy law. Sometimes his very name 'Moses' is used in the New Testament when the speaker is really referring to the law (John 5:45). So here came the consummate law-giver, God's instrument of judgement, who thus far only had one covenant instruction to observe, namely to circumcise his son – but he hadn't done so. The one who will require absolute obedience was disobedient at home. He was disqualified! In fact, he was as good as dead. Swift action by Zipporah dealt with the area of compromise and presumption. Mercy immediately followed. 'He left him alone.'

This episode in the life of Moses is full of lessons for us, maybe more important than any other since it was actually life-threatening. The future law-giver was in fact a law-breaker at home. What he would require publicly, he wasn't owning privately. His personal compromise thoroughly disqualified him in God's eyes.

So why the disobedient neglect of such a clear requirement from God? Maybe one clue was Zipporah's reaction. She clearly hated the rite of circumcision and though she quickly performed the act, presumably because Moses was near death's door, she was appalled by it. Not a Hebrew herself, she didn't embrace the concept. Perhaps on the eighth day, when the boy should have been circumcised, she had withstood Moses. Maybe he disobeyed God in order to keep the peace at home.

It's very striking that God didn't even have to point out their area of disobedience. Nothing was identified by him. They knew immediately what the problem was.

Anything like that in your life? Something you know that God hates, but you put up with? It needs to go, and quickly! Ruthlessly! Even if there will be ramifications with others who perhaps share in your disobedience.

Maybe just looking after a few sheep in a wilderness meant that zeal had faded, standards had dropped. Now he was called by God, who wanted a pure instrument, a man who could confront Pharaoh and act on his behalf. Internal, secret disobedience doesn't qualify you for God's service and make you strong in the battle. A troubled conscience will always undermine in the conflict. However, if we confess our sins, He is faithful and just to forgive us our sins and cleanse us from all unrighteousness. Will you take action and sort things out?

I love the way Exodus Chapter 4 ends. Aaron, the future High Priest, came to meet the chastened Moses, embraced and kissed him and they walked on together. Jesus, our great Priest, will do the same when we repent and turn from sin. His personal embrace is so tender towards the genuinely penitent and the joy of walking on in his company is what we were called to.[4] His embrace and his fellowship heals, restores and fits us for the task.

A chapter which began with such reluctance ends with a man set free and ready for all that lies ahead. Now the story can begin.

6

Why did you ever send me?

Advances and setbacks. Exodus 5.

Now the story really starts. Or does it? Certainly, it begins with a flourish! Moses sounds like a mighty Old Testament prophet. With frightening authority, he demanded of Pharaoh, 'Thus says the Lord, the God of Israel, let my people go!' Wow, really impressive! Except sadly it's water off a duck's back to almighty Pharaoh. Shockingly he was completely indifferent and dismissive to Moses' appeal. 'Who is the Lord that I should obey His voice? I do not know the Lord and I will not let Israel go' (Exod. 5:2). That certainly was not what Moses expected. Pharaoh proved to be a formidable opponent, certainly no pushover.

Moses has run at speed into a brick wall. What now? He slightly changed his tone in the next verse. Rather less demanding, maybe a little more conciliatory, 'Please let us go on a three-day's journey into the wilderness that we might sacrifice…' It does rather sound like he's floundering.

Pharaoh was unmoved. Not only rock-like in his refusal, even spiteful in his reaction. He regarded Moses' God-inspired appeal as a cheap endeavour to let the slaves off their workload. They clearly needed to learn a lesson. Not only were they not to be allowed their freedom, their workload would be severely increased. Bricks to be made without being provided with the necessary straw. Let them gather the straw themselves, but maintain the same productivity.

Wait a minute! This wasn't what Moses anticipated. He was there with a divine commission. He had learned his lesson about running ahead of God. Now he was God's man doing God's work, and it was a disaster! What's going on?

Is this such a rare occurrence in biblical narrative? In Isaiah 61:1, God promised that a glorious anointed one would come to bind up the broken-hearted, proclaim freedom to the captives and release prisoners. A promise of a wonderful new day. A day then came at the synagogue in Nazareth when one stood and said, 'Today this Scripture has been fulfilled in your hearing'. At last the promise fulfilled. Jesus, having waited thirty years, had stepped on to the public stage. But who would have predicted the reaction? Instead of celebrating his arrival, they tried to push him off a nearby cliff!

Later the apostles, obeying the risen and now exalted Christ, began to share the good news of a Messiah who had overcome death and was now on David's throne with all authority in heaven and on earth. Initial breakthrough was rapidly followed by implacable hostility. Having courageously declared that there was no other name under heaven by which we must be saved, the response was, don't you dare to speak another word in that name! Beatings and imprisonment followed.

Later, Paul, perplexed about his next preaching location, received supernatural guidance. 'Come over to Macedonia and help us' (Acts 6:9), a call to Europe. At last it was now clear! They were plainly on course and in God's will, but within such a short space of time he and Silas are in the inner prison with their backs bleeding from the beating they had endured. It can be so perplexing to be obedient to God, as far as you know, only to meet an air-sapping punch in the solar plexus.

Perhaps you've felt stirred to be open and honest at your

workplace and grabbed what looked like a God-given opportunity to witness to your faith, only to find not only rejection, but a new reputation among your work colleagues as a 'holy Joe', someone to be avoided at the lunch or coffee break. Not an advance, but an apparent setback.

Bewildered, Moses felt like abandoning all hope. A chapter which began so impressively ended with his forlorn cry, 'Why did you ever send me?' He had gone expecting breakthrough and not only encountered a hostile Pharaoh, but his own people turned against him again. 'May the Lord look on you and judge you' (Exod. 5:21) they shout. 'You've made our situation so much worse.'

Back to God

When you hit this kind of obstacle and deep disappointment, you need to learn the lessons and walk wisely. Moses did exactly the right thing. He went back to God with his complaint, as the psalmist did on many occasions. At such times we become perplexed on several levels. Emotionally we can feel that God let us down. We can experience profound pain, even devastation. Moses didn't bottle up his feelings, he took them back to God. Why did this happen to me? Why didn't you do what you promised?

You must beware Satan's cunning. He always tries to separate you from God, suggesting that God is not really to be trusted. We feel we can't call God a liar and so try to crush the emotional pain inside of us. Moses did much better than that. He took his complaint to God. Many psalms start with the psalmist questioning and apparently complaining, but result in fresh encounters with God and renewed faith and confidence.

We are not called to a kind of stoical endurance. We are called to personal fellowship with the living God. We are not meant to press on with the proverbial British stiff upper lip; we are allowed to ask questions, express frustrations. Don't slink away from Him at such times, run to Him with your questions. Don't subscribe to a formal stance which says that we know God is faithful, that's the official line, but let's face it, in reality He isn't. He lets you down. That is Satan's whisper. Refuse it!

Actually, there was an answer.

Moses had not listened carefully at his time of commissioning. He failed to read the small print. God had told him (Exod. 3:19), 'But I know that the King of Egypt will not permit you to go except under compulsion'. Somehow Moses had missed that caveat. A delay was going to take place. God's awesome power was going to be displayed through a series of unprecedented signs and wonders. Actually, Moses, in deep despair, was completely in the centre of God's will. All was well. From God's point of view, he was completely on course, even though he felt so bereft and broken.

Apparent setbacks and disappointments that seem to break your heart can actually be blessings in disguise. You rarely see the whole picture clearly. Also, the story is so much bigger than the part you personally play. You must learn to trust and obey even when you don't understand. If you experience constant success and every Pharaoh fell to his knees before you, you might start assuming some really dangerous things about yourself. If your path was never rocky and difficult, you might miss the point entirely. Apparent setbacks and even heartbreaks can work God's purpose in you as you learn patience and begin to understand that it's ultimately His story not yours.

James develops the theme so helpfully in his letter in the New Testament. He tells you to consider it all joy when you encounter various trials, knowing that the testing of your faith produces endurance and endurance must have its perfect result that you may be perfect and complete, lacking nothing.

These were still early days in Moses' journey and a painful lesson had been learned. In our next chapter, God will step out of the shadows and make an awesome statement of intent and His predetermined purpose will certainly come to pass. Like the Apostle Paul, the deflated Moses will learn not to trust in himself, but in God who raises the dead (2 Cor. 1:9).

7

I will take you for my people

God chooses us. Exodus 6:1–12

Moses, deflated and confused, turned back to God. His efforts had failed. The plan had apparently come to nothing. Immediately he experienced an even more awesome encounter, not with the arrogant yet ignorant Pharaoh, but with the unstoppable God whose purpose was unaffected by an apparent setback. Nothing had changed. No need for any adjustment of His plans. From Moses' perspective all looked lost, but God didn't suffer from self-doubt or insecurity about what he could perform.

Pharaoh had arrogantly enquired, 'Who is the Lord?' and completely undermined Moses' confidence, yet God was about to remind Moses precisely who he was and what he was about to do.

Hollywood never has quite understood what the story of Moses and the exodus was about. Freeing slaves from terrible oppression makes a dramatic story, especially with plagues and a Red Sea opening thrown in. But the story of the book of Exodus unveils so much more. It's an extended answer to the question, 'Who is the Lord that I should obey him?' God wasn't simply rescuing slaves, which was of course remarkable in itself, but he was giving one of the most dramatic demonstrations of His identity, his power and his ultimate purpose, namely to have a people for Himself.

Actually, the chief end of God in the creation of man was to have a special people of whom he could say, 'I am theirs and they are mine'. There is in scripture no phrase more frequent or more fundamental in its disclosure of God's purpose than variations of the declaration, 'I will be to them a God, and they shall be to me a people'.

God had spoken to Abraham, Isaac and Jacob about the unique nature of the family they would produce. Now a growing nation made up of twelve tribes had multiplied and was going to emerge as that people, a unique nation on the earth to whom, and through whom, God would manifest His glory.

Completely undaunted, God gave Moses fresh instructions. Now he was to become as God to Pharaoh and Aaron was to be his spokesman, or his prophet speaking on Moses' behalf (Exod. 7:1). The strategy was becoming more explicit. God would harden Pharaoh's heart so that he would multiply his signs and wonders. God would bring His people out with great judgements and Egypt would know that he was the Lord. An extended series of plagues would follow that would humble Egypt and demonstrate God's majesty and awesome power.

A man under authority

Initially Pharaoh's magicians would apparently match Moses' extraordinary signs, but before long Moses' signs are completely out of their league. Initially, Moses was easily dismissed, but he gradually grew in stature and authority. By repeatedly returning to the Lord after his frustrating encounters with Pharaoh, he acted as a true prophet, a man under authority genuinely representing God and acting together with God, who magnificently owned Moses' words. Repeatedly, Moses did exactly according to the word of the Lord, until we read the extraordinary words, 'The

Lord did according to the word of Moses' (Exod. 8:13). Plagues were threatened, executed and accomplished their purpose as Moses repeatedly encountered Pharaoh, then returned to God for further instructions so that ultimately Moses was greatly esteemed in the land of Egypt, both in the sight of Pharaoh's servants and in the sight of the people (Exod. 11:3). Moses' authority and presence seemed to multiply as Pharaoh's diminished.

Before Moses left Egypt, his and Pharaoh's status were transformed, with Pharaoh asking Moses to bless him (Exod. 12:32). God had sustained His servant through the battering and perplexing process, and now he stood vindicated as the servant of God with all of God's breathtaking resources behind him.

We, the modern church, must learn this lesson. When we encounter frustrating roadblocks and the refusal of our contemporary culture, it is not for us to adjust our message or abandon our calling. Like Moses, we must always come back to God and stay true to His word. The world waits to encounter a church that comes fresh from meetings with God and, as a result, speaks with God's authority. Elijah would later speak with the authority of one who stood in the presence of God (I Kings 17:1). Our authority does not come from our personal eloquence – it comes uniquely from the authority of the one on whose behalf we speak.

8

The Passover

A new age, a new meal. Exodus 12:1–30.

Plague after frightening plague culminated in the most dreadful of all, the one to be remembered in Jewish culture throughout the generations. It was to mark the end of slavery and the 'beginning of months' for Israel (Exod. 12:2). A new age was dawning. Pharaoh had repeatedly refused the warnings and demonstrations of God's power, and now the ultimate judgement would pass on his nation. The combination of God's compassion for Israel's slaves and fury at Egypt's cold indifference and obstinacy was about to be unleashed. The firstborn of every family would die in one night.

Like Noah's ark, the Passover provided safety for the present storm and the promise of life in the future. Terrifying judgement was literally at their door, but the congregation of Israel was shown a means of escape. What happened surpassed a slave rescue, it was a revelation of God. Modern news reports of large-scale disasters borrow the phrase 'of biblical proportions', the ramifications of the event they are describing reminiscent of the vastness of biblical stories. Yet we need full exposure to biblical narrative to inform our view of God. J. I. Packer has said, 'Today vast stress is laid on the thought that God is personal, but this truth is so stated as to leave the impression that God is a person of the same sort as we are.'[5] The account of Egypt's plagues provides a shocking wake up call for us. God is altogether other than us, He rules over His creation. At His command plagues overwhelm Egypt; thousands of frogs, insects and gnats are summoned, pestilence wipes out livestock, soot created boils, hail followed by thunder and fire, and swarms of locusts follow, and even the light of the sun is obscured for three days.

God performed all these signs and wonders in order to show His power and proclaim His name throughout all the earth (Exod. 9:16). The more His name is truly known, honoured and glorified, the more everybody benefits. Everyone suffers when we develop and become comfortable with an inadequate view of God. This awesome display of His power was answering Pharaoh's arrogant question, 'Who is the Lord that I should obey him?'

Pharaoh's problem remains in our modern society, leading to flagrant disregard for His righteous requirements and gross dismissiveness of the Saviour that He sent and the gospel He proclaimed.

However, the final plague not only provided the harshest judgement, it also delivered a glorious escape route for the slave community. All the firstborn of every Egyptian family would die in one night, from Pharaoh's household to the lowliest slave's home, so that a great cry was heard throughout the whole land because there was no home free from death. God demonstrated His righteous judgement on a vast scale.

At the same time, He revealed to Moses and the nation of Israel His means of escape for them. Blood had to be shed for each household. An unblemished lamb had to be selected and killed, and blood had to be sprinkled on the outer doorposts of every home. The blood of the lamb would substitute for the firstborn of the family. Because the lamb died, their firstborn could live. The promise was given that, when he saw the blood, he would pass over that family. It was vital for them to understand that the blood of the lamb was for God to see; it was not for them to gaze upon and ponder. They were to be inside the house, actually eating the lamb. Only God knew the importance and value of the blood of the lamb.

Christ our Passover

All this, of course, is hugely relevant to us as Christian believers whose confidence is in Jesus, the lamb of God who takes away the sin of the world (John 1:29). We who are justified by His blood must not spend our time wondering if the blood of the lamb is sufficient to cover our sins. It was not for the Hebrews to keep running outside their homes to look at the blood and try to feel its worth in order to steady their fears. God did not urge them to gaze on the blood, He plainly said, 'When I see the blood'. The blood is for God to see. Only He knows its true worth. Only He comprehends what this shed blood has accomplished. Our peace comes not from trying to analyse, but from understanding that God is satisfied, His wrath is turned away. We have peace because He is propitiated. Being justified by faith in the shed blood of the lamb, we have peace with God.

From this beginning, this inauguration of a new age in their experience, the Hebrews were always to commemorate this event. The night of The Passover was to hold a central place in their sense of identity. Each year they should gather in their homes with their families to celebrate The Passover, the day the lamb died that they might be saved – the whole nation should remember on the same evening. It should be no surprise to us that Jesus was crucified at Passover time when thousands had gathered in Jerusalem to celebrate the feast. At the very Passover feast with his family of disciples, he inaugurated the promised new covenant in his blood shed for many for the forgiveness of sins.

Now we no longer kill a lamb. Our lamb was slain once for all, but the power of his blood is such that all our sins are washed away. God the Father has made peace with us through the blood of His son. Christ our Passover is sacrificed for us (1 Cor. 5:7).

The blood of Jesus actually cleanses our conscience. We need no longer fear judgement or rejection, or even wrestle with inward condemnation. Because his blood has been shed, there is therefore now no condemnation for those in Christ Jesus. Judgement has passed. This will be spelt out in far more detail in the instructions given in the book of Leviticus, but here at the birth of the nation the slain Passover lambs point the way. And because Christ our Passover is sacrificed for us, we can go free from our captivity (1 Cor. 5:7).

9

Follow the cloud

Finding your path, God's way. Exodus 13:20–22,
14:21–31

Early Christians were called followers of the way, an unusual title, but surely one that spoke of a people not static but on the move, not on a random journey but one of significance and purpose. The Israelites had been slaves for years, living a life void of movement; travel was not part of their experience. As slaves they were going nowhere.

From now on, life would be different in so many ways. Now they were a people on the move, with all the new dangers and perils that travelling entailed. Stagnation would be left behind, but navigating the unknown presented new perplexities and challenges. Happily, God gave them a simple solution to the problem. Follow the cloud. A supernatural cloud would go before them, even glowing with light at night. They were not called upon to dream up strategies or to plan their route, they were called simply to follow.

Being a follower is such a basic description of a believer's identity and calling. Jesus' first words in gathering the young church were, 'Follow me and I will make you...' (Matthew 4:19). We have a leader who told us that one of his names is 'the way'. Being a follower implies trust in the leader, letting him make the choices with the implication that he knows best.

Sometimes the route can be perplexing and our attitude at such times reveals the degree to which our trust in his wisdom and love are established. The journey that Israel took as they followed the cloud was not a predictable one. Although a nearby route beckoned them, we are told that the cloud led them 'around the way of the wilderness' (Exod. 13:17). This provided an early chance to ask questions and challenge the wisdom of that decision. Yet the story lets us into the secret of God's motivation. He was leading them on a path that would avoid war.

We rarely see the full picture.

It is so good to follow one who knows what is round the next corner. We might be tempted to form an opinion based on our limited knowledge. In fact, God's guidance was based both on His knowledge and His compassion. Ephesians 1 speaks of 'the mystery of His will' (Eph. 1:9), but also tells us of 'the kind intention of His will' (Eph. 1:5). Following the cloud provides security and makes perfect sense when we trust the character of the one leading. The path might be mysterious, but it's never random. As God guides us, He will always be true to himself. The longer you have walked with him, the more you will have reason to trust His guidance.

Years later, through the prophet Hosea, God said, 'When Israel was a child, I loved him and out of Egypt I called my son... It was I who taught Ephraim to walk, taking him by the arms, but they didn't realise it was I who healed them. I led them with the cords of human kindness, with ties of love. I lifted the yoke from their neck and bent down to feed them' (Hos. 11:1, 3, 4). Those of us who have taught our children to walk will recognize the parental compassion and delight involved.

When we follow, we relinquish our right to choose. Prior to conversion we made our own choices, walked our own path. Being a follower requires a different perspective. Like the Israelites, we don't always learn this overnight. We have our own personal preferences. Following the cloud is a lesson to be learned, a lifestyle to be cultivated.

Recognizing guidance

But what does the cloud look like in our world? How do we know which way to go? I have learned to trust my car's satellite navigation, as its instructions are remarkably clear. Many Christians find guidance complicated. Jesus said simply, 'My sheep hear my voice and follow me' (John 10:4). That sounds so simple, but it is not as simple as my sat-nav. With that I already know my desired destination and simply have to press a few buttons. Following Jesus requires other factors in place. For one, I don't necessarily know the destination from the start, and I certainly don't know every turning on the road.

Abraham, the forerunner of all who believe, was invited to leave home, family and all that was familiar and secure to go simply to 'the land I will show you'. 'Where is that then?' he might have asked, and I guess the answer would have been, 'I will show you'. Naked trust was implicit in his taking the journey.

When Jesus called his early disciples, he simply invited them to follow him and thoroughly trust him to guide. Some were unwilling to risk the potential danger and loss. Others could say we've left all to follow you. Following Christ is not a casual thing – abandonment to his will is involved. If we are reluctant to be led, or want our own particular preferences, we will become confused, but guidance will come to those who are clearly willing to be his sheep and want him to be their shepherd. He has promised. Sometimes we are baffled by the choices that lie before us, but that's not time to doubt his shepherding love and commitment to guide.

Later, Moses would be told to ascend the mountain and there God would speak to him. Having ascended, we are told that ten days later God spoke to him. I think having climbed a mountain to meet God he might speak to me straight away, but I need to remember that he is God and I am not. I am His servant. I might need to wait. So it is with guidance. You might have to wait, but He will guide.

Following Him means travelling at His pace, not enforcing ours on him. Not rushing ahead or lagging behind. On my part, I know He led me to leave my secular job, through a growing longing in my heart to serve him, culminating in a weekend where He spoke very clearly. Then He surprised me by telling me to go to Bible College, something I was determined never to do. Yet seven people over two or three weeks individually and independently suggested it to me. I thought I would have to be very arrogant to ignore seven people, so I rather reluctantly pushed some doors. They opened rather spectacularly and I was convinced God was guiding. I felt God led me to the girl I was to marry. Initially she withstood my advances. Three days of prayer and fasting that God would either get her to change her mind or get her out of my hair, led to her turning around. After fifty years of marriage we have never doubted we were led together.

In my last year at theological college I had no idea where we were to go. Several offers and suggestions were made and I sensed a very clear 'no' from God, but where? In my final college vacation, with ten weeks to go, an invitation came and God made the way clear. Looking back over 64 years of Christian experience, I can honestly say the Lord has led continually. Sometimes I would have been more comfortable if I had known earlier. Guidance came at the last minute, faith has been tested, but He has wonderfully led.

On the other hand, we mustn't become too precious about guidance. Some things are plainly His will. We need no special word. For instance, we are to give thanks in all circumstances for that is the will of God (1 Thess. 5:18). We are also to do what is right (2 Pet. 1:15) – no guidance is needed there, and simply observing that truth will quickly resolve some choices that have to be made. If we determine not to be conformed to this world, but be transformed by the renewing of our mind, we shall come to prove what is the will of God which is good, acceptable and perfect (see Rom. 12:2).

Remember that, although the route may be unexpected to you, God is not making it up as He goes along. You are His workmanship, created in Christ Jesus for works that He prepared beforehand for you to walk in (Eph. 2:10). What a privilege! Keep following the cloud.

10

A frightening road block

God, and impossible opposition. Exodus 14:1–31

The Red Sea crossing stands as one of the most famous stories in the Bible, foundational to the identity of the Jewish nation. Yet immediately prior to that extraordinary event, life looked very different. Israel, following God's guidance provided by the cloud, had arrived at a complete dead end. The Red Sea blocked their way. Surely, they were following God and now at an impasse. Not only that, the Egyptian army was hot on their heels. When following supernatural guidance, you don't anticipate a cul-de-sac.

Some fascinating attitudes now surfaced which are worth noting. First, Pharaoh jumped to a conclusion typical of those who don't know God. His view of things was that the Israelites were 'wandering aimlessly... and the wilderness has shut them in' (Exod. 14:3). In spite of the plagues, his hardened heart refused to believe that Israel's God could actually deliver the slave nation. Stubborn unbelief refused to face facts. Hardened hearts always dismiss what is plain to see. When Jesus healed the man born blind, his opponents refused to acknowledge plain reality. When Lazarus was raised from the dead, Jesus' most remarkable miracle, instead of being stunned, they planned not only to kill Jesus, but Lazarus as well (John 12:10).

Paul tells us in 1 Corinthians 2:14 that the man without the

Spirit doesn't accept the things that are from God. They are foolishness to him, he can't understand them. Pharaoh's unbelief forced him to put his own interpretation on events: they are wandering aimlessly. Believers have often been dismissed in a similar fashion by their unbelieving contemporaries. Spiritual realities are refuted as foolishness, to be dismissed by the wise of this world. Pharaoh continued in his arrogance. He was yet to discover that the foolishness of God is wiser than men (1 Cor. 1:25). He was thinking on a natural plane, and kicking himself that he had let Israel go from serving Egypt (Exod. 14:5).

Having said that, the Israelites were not exactly brimming with faith and courage. Rather the opposite, they became very frightened (Exod. 14:10). Fear is a powerful enemy with devastating impact. It drained their strength. It completely distracted them from their course of action. It made them get everything out of proportion. It made them forget the things that they knew and had recently experienced. It made foolish alternatives look attractive, arguing it would have been better to remain in Egypt and be slaves to the Egyptians. Fear distorted everything. The slave community immediately forgot the amazing signs and wonders they had just experienced. They failed to be sustained by the demonstration of God's powerful protective hand upon them in delivering them from the terrifying plagues. Fear is a powerful enemy. It is intuitive. We all experience it, but we must learn to manage it.

I once heard Billy Graham testify that he had been in an aeroplane suddenly in danger. He said that as a believer he was not automatically indifferent to the situation. His immediate reaction was fear, which he said is an appropriate human response. We are not automatically fearless as though our natural instincts are blanked out as Christians. No, he had to pause, pray, consider, remember and reflect on truth so that he could, as a believer, replace his natural reaction to one based on the truth that he knew about life, death and a Saviour.

Fear had to be mastered. Moses said to the people, 'Don't fear!', a command often repeated in Scripture. Fear is instinctive and powerful, but as believers it does not have to win the day in our lives. We have reason not to fear. God had made them promises, was leading them and was able to handle the situation. As their shepherd, he was responsible for them and would care for them, which he did in spectacular fashion.

Trust God to guide

Paul tells us, in 1 Corinthians 10:11, that these things happened to them as an example and were written down for our instruction. The people of God actually experienced this journey. God actually looked after them and the details are written to instruct us. God can be trusted. God who leads into challenging situations does not abandon us there. If we have followed His leading, we are His responsibility, He will see us through. The Hebrews were told not to fear, but to stand firm and see God's salvation.

So many times, in God's mercy, I have experienced God's awesome interventions when the way looked completely blocked. All we could do was look to God, stand firm and see His salvation. If you run for it, you see nothing, but if you obey God when He says 'stand firm', you see God.

I remember, as a young and inexperienced pastor, being confronted by an unhappy season in the church I was serving. Although I had been clearly led there, we were encountering such setbacks, even strong disagreements at leadership level. My wife and I were dismayed. Despondency grew. How could God bless such disunity? Eventually I sat and carefully wrote my letter of resignation, expressing my frustration. We would leave. As I finished it and read it through, I heard God's voice in my heart, 'Did I tell you to write that?'. As I sat in silence, I knew He hadn't. I threw it away. Later, God wonderfully intervened.

We often associate faith with courageous, adventurous steps, maybe into the unknown, but faith is sometimes allied with patiently waiting. It isn't manifested by finding a way out and running for it. Too often, when delay occurs, we are tempted to take things into our own hands and abandon the path God has provided. We need to learn to stand still and see the salvation of God. Over the years, I have sadly met a number of pastors who have moved on so many times that they can't remember when they last knew they were in the will of God.

We really need to hear God say, 'don't fear' in the same way that we hear Him say 'don't steal, don't lie, don't commit adultery'. It is a command. Don't do it! Don't live there. Don't accommodate it. Yet it has to be replaced by something else. We have to trust God, believe Him and reverence Him in all His power, wisdom and love.

What was about to happen was one of the most magnificent displays of God's power in the whole Bible. God who had heard their cry, seen their predicament as slaves, had come down to deliver them. He had already displayed breathtaking power in signs and wonders through the devastating plagues. He had then led them spectacularly by a cloud to this point. He was not going to abandon them there. They were His responsibility. He would see them through.

If you have arrived at a road block through foolishly taking the wrong turning, disobeying God and going off on your own, you need to repent and turn back to where you know you were genuinely following God, ask His forgiveness and get back on His road. If you know that God has led you and that you have simply been obedient, you must stand still and see God's salvation.

11

The song of Moses

I will sing to the Lord! Exodus 15:1–21

Exodus 15 is undoubtedly one of the greatest songs of worship in
the Bible. Moses, exhilarated by the breathtaking display of God's
power and the realization that God had devastated their enemies and
thoroughly liberated them, broke into song and all Israel joined in.
All praise was directed to Yahweh. He had done it! They were helpless,
threatened and thoroughly endangered, but God had demonstrated
both His awesome power and His jealous love for His people by a
glorious miracle. He opened the sea so that they could walk through
on dry ground and then enveloped their enemies, allowing the
waters to thunder down upon them in their hostile pursuit. The
sensational event not only secured their salvation, it granted an
awe-inspiring revelation of who this God is. He meant business and
nothing at all could stop Him and His magnificent purpose.

The event led to an explosion of worship, such a vital dimension
in the lives of God's people. True worship is motivated not by
religious duty, but by a revelation of God. This was the first outburst
of corporate praise in the Bible. It followed an extraordinary
revelation of who God is and how much He loved His people and
would act on their behalf. Moses sounds like he is bursting with
joy and excitement when he sings and shouts, 'Yahweh is a warrior!
...they sank like lead!' He can't contain his sense of wonder at the
God of his salvation.

They worshipped because they saw what God had done and got to know Him like they had never known Him before. Later in Israel's history there would come a similar outburst of worship when Israel was freed to make its way back to their homeland from the Babylonish captivity, 'When the Lord turned again the captivity of Zion, we were like those that dream. Then our mouth was filled with laughter and our tongue with joyful shouting' (Psalm 126:1, 2).

The situation had been bleak and indeed terrifying. Moses' song included reference to the impending danger. The enemy said, 'I will pursue, I will overtake. I will divide the spoil... I will draw my sword; my hand will destroy them!' (Exod. 15:9). Pharaoh's chariots and horsemen must have been a horrifying sight. Destruction must have looked inevitable. The facts spoke for themselves. A defenceless crowd of slaves with neither chariots, horses or swords was pursued by a fully equipped army.

Yet the initial command was, 'Don't fear! Stand still and see the salvation of Yahweh which He will accomplish for you today... The Lord will fight for you.' Although things outwardly looked so impossible, God was in control and a very present help in time of trouble. His next command was, 'Tell the sons of Israel to go forward!' (Exod. 14:15). Moses was then told to take his staff and stretch it out and divide the sea. Would they hold their nerve or disintegrate with fear? God's authoritative voice, 'Out of Egypt I called my Son' (Hosea 11:1), needed a responsive and obedient heart. The nation, which was in a sense to be born out of water like any child, was to be born by faith. Faith was to characterize them as a people. Moses, by faith, raised his staff and the Lord swept the sea back. The door to freedom swung open. God's glory was revealed. Out of Egypt He called His Son.

Faith and obedience bring revelation

Members of the early church were often called 'believers' and acted as such. Without faith it is impossible to please God or indeed to advance on the Christian journey. If we twenty-first century Christians are to see apparently closed doors open, we must rediscover the great weapon of faith. So often we are urged simply to use our common sense or to face the facts so that the way forward is impossible. This pragmatism has to be overcome. As we have seen, these great stories were written down not simply to entertain, but so that we can learn from them. I am so grateful that on many occasions I have seen apparently impenetrable doors burst open as people have refused to yield to fear and have advanced by faith.

Moses shouted, 'You blew with your wind, the sea covered them, they sank like lead! Your right-hand O Yahweh is majestic in power, your right hand shatters the enemy. Who is like you among the gods O Yahweh? Who is like you majestic in holiness, awesome in praises, doing wonders!' It's hard to miss the sense of wonder and awe mixed with profound gratitude for the deliverance they had experienced. What seemed inescapable peril was transformed into complete deliverance.

If we don't believe, we shall see nothing. When we believe and obediently advance, God's power is released, His glory is revealed leading to bursts of worship.

The church must line up with these biblical characters and emulate their faith, or we shall simply decline. These were flesh and blood people facing frightening odds who discovered that God would step in for them and act on their behalf.

Satan knocks and taunts individuals with his insinuations that they are trapped and hopeless, still slaves, still not free. Cruelly he argues, 'Maybe you have sheltered under the Passover blood. Maybe you have experienced forgiveness, but you will never be free from the chains I have put around you. You are still captive to your fierce temper, bondage to fear, lustful habits, pornography. You know you will never be free,' he whispers, 'you are still my slave.'

We don't overcome by willpower, nor by simply 'letting go and letting God', as some would have it. We are called to advance by faith. The crossing of the Red Sea marked the beginning of Israel as a nation. It was as though they were buried and rose again on the other side. This imagery underlines Paul's New Testament argument in Romans 6. To the Christian who asks, 'Shall we continue in sin? Am I still a captive?' he replies, 'By no means! How can he who died to sin still live in it?' He then goes on to argue that we who have been baptized into Christ have been baptized into his death. He continues, 'Therefore we have been buried with him through baptism into death, so that as Christ was raised from the dead through the glory of the Father, so we too might walk in newness of life' (Rom. 6:4). We are beyond the Red Sea. Paul confidently declares that we are no longer slaves to sin. Our old man was crucified with Christ and we are free. When Satan tries to lie to you that you are still his slave, maybe you should ask him how many Egyptian soldiers survived the Red Sea! No, they were free! By advancing by faith and obedience they were on dry ground on the other side.

No wonder God's people celebrated! No wonder they sang! Jesus said knowing the truth sets us free, so we need to know that all of us who have been baptized into Christ have been baptized into his death. As we consider this to be the truth and reckon on our new identity in Christ as no longer a slave, we shall walk more and more into the freedom that he has provided. Israel were former slaves, now free. So it is for believers in Christ, his death and resurrection. Let's celebrate the freedom he has won for us and walk on with him in a journey that yet has many more discoveries.

12

Bitterness encountered and overcome

God will refresh you. Exodus 15:22–27

Should we be amazed at the Israelites' fickleness? Perhaps, if we are getting to know ourselves, we shouldn't be. It seems that so quickly after their excitement and celebration of deliverance they started to grumble (Exod. 15:24). It is sad to find this account tucked into the same chapter as Moses' triumphant song. Surely it could have waited for another chapter? Yet the Bible is alarmingly realistic. It's God's book and He knows our human frame. He remembers that we are dust (Psalm 103:14). We can so easily lurch from exhilaration to disillusionment and devastation. These freshly delivered slaves had much to learn, even as we have as we continue our journey in these 'ends of the ages'. They went out into the wilderness (Exod. 15:22) and after three days they found no water. I guess one day might just be bearable, but by day two perhaps cries could be heard, 'What about the children?' By day three terror may have begun to sweep through the advancing two million. What would become of them? The pillar of cloud beckoned them on, but it was not providing what they actually needed.

In the same way, the young Christian can also be frightened and admit that this isn't what was expected. I thought life would be so different, easier. New birth was so exciting. I never knew anything like it before. I now belong to God. My sins are forgiven. God is leading me, but sadly serious challenges still face me. I never anticipated that people would start backing off me at work, saying I've 'gone religious'. And actually, I never thought I would meet Christians who would let me down and even say unkind things. At first everybody was so excited that I had become a Christian, but now some have already let me down. Some even seem cliquey. I can't seem to get into their circle.

Not only that, I don't seem to be as changed as I thought I would be. Can I honestly live without some of the things that I used to do, but now as a Christian I shouldn't? I still find myself unhappy and recently I lost my temper. Disappointment can assail us. We can begin to wonder, have I really got what it takes to live the Christian life?

The Israelites plainly wondered how they were going to cope. You can only go without water for a limited time. Then at last a ripple of hope ran through the vast crowd. News was being passed back. They had found water up ahead at Marah. Thank God the trial was over; thank goodness our thirst will soon be quenched. Then, utter horror. Marah's water was bitter! Undrinkable! Hopes raised, only to be dashed, are worse than having no hope at all. The house sale that looks secure falls through, the job interview that looked so promising comes to nothing. The boyfriend/girlfriend you began to build your hopes on drops you. Deep disappointment can be hard to manage. Bitterness is waiting at your door.

The temptation to abandon the cloud must have been great. What's the point of guidance if you are only led to disappointment and heartbreak? Alternatives like taking a different path or becoming cynical about the whole thing come clamouring into your mind. Another alternative is simply to grumble at those who are supposed to be leading. Maybe the Israelites couldn't complain directly to God, but they 'grumbled at Moses' (Exod. 15:24). The leader felt the pressure. Suddenly he was the one to blame.

The Lord showed him a tree

Understandably, we read that Moses cried out to the Lord. What follows is quite striking. It doesn't say, 'he saw a tree', it actually says, 'the Lord showed him a tree which he threw into the waters which then became sweet' (Exod. 15:25). The tree seemed to have extraordinary healing powers. Down through the centuries, Christian commentators, such as the famous Matthew Henry, and preachers have brought a Christian perspective to the story. The Cross is often referred to as a tree in the New Testament. For instance, Peter accuses his hearers of 'hanging him on a tree' (Acts 5:30; see also Acts 10:39 and Gal. 3:13), and undoubtedly Christians understand that the Cross fully revealed has awesome power to heal. Of course, as Christians we see power in the Cross that is not seen by those who reject the gospel. To them the Cross is mere foolishness. Yet to those who believe and have had its power revealed to them, it is the power of God (1 Cor. 1:18). However, we need to learn how to apply it to our circumstances.

As a fairly young Christian I recall planning to attend the famous Keswick Convention, held annually in England's Lake District. I lived in Brighton on the south coast and had been driving a motor scooter for some years. Until now I had driven it exclusively around town. To be honest, that is what is expected of such a means of transport. I had recently returned from a season of backsliding and summer holidays had formerly been the setting for outrageous activity. I determined to radically change my life. I had never attended a Christian conference before and decided with my friend to go to Keswick on my scooter. It seemed a truly Christian thing to do, almost like a sacred pilgrimage. Scooters were not really manufactured with such long journeys in mind. We set off and after some long hours found ourselves crossing the Peak District. It was bleak and hilly, with no place to stop, rest or, indeed, shelter. Gradually the skies filled with ever-darker clouds. Suddenly rain and hail poured down on us. I had no helmet or gloves and was completely vulnerable to the dreadful downpour. It seemed the piercing hailstones were deliberately directed to my defenceless hands, face and particularly my eyes. It seemed like torture and this on my sacred pilgrimage! Why wasn't God protecting me? As my hands and head hurt, I was suddenly reminded of the Cross. I thought of Christ's hands and face. I shouted my thoughts to my friend as we drove along. What about Jesus, his hands, his head. We began to celebrate and sing as we drove through the storm. It was truly remarkable. The bitterness had disappeared, replaced by wonder and worship. The Cross not only saves you at the outset of your Christian life. If you learn to throw it into the bitter water it makes it sweet. We need to run our race fixing our eyes on Jesus, the author and perfecter of faith who, for the joy set before him, endured the Cross and despised the shame (Hebrews 12:3–7). Consider him who endured such hostility by sinners against himself lest you grow weary and faint in your mind.

I once had the privilege of sitting with a Chinese pastor in Shanghai who had spent twenty-one years in jail for his commitment to Christ. Taken from his wife and six children when he was forty-four years old, he was released aged sixty-five. I said to him, 'You have suffered so much in following Christ.' I shall never forget the radiance of his face as he replied simply, 'Nothing compares with the Cross.' His spirit was free, not a trace of bitterness.

13

Daily manna for the journey

God's Goodness in our Grumbling. Exodus 16.

By now you might hope to find some moral progress in the delivered slave community, but sadly there is little to encourage. Our next chapter opens with further complaints being expressed by God's people. Water had been graciously provided, but what about food? How were they going to survive without something to eat? No maturity on display yet as they immediately started complaining again. Drawing on their distorted, nostalgic memories of the good old days when they used to 'sit by the meat pots and eat bread to the full' (Exod. 16:2), they recalled the balmy days of their captivity.

Years of slavery had produced shrivelled souls apparently incapable of a positive appreciation of their new situation. Undoubtedly used to complaining in their former life, they failed to take into account their changed circumstances. The Israelites simply switched the focus of their complaints from their previous masters to start murmuring about Moses. They had physically escaped slavery in Egypt, but sadly they had brought their slave culture with them. Life in captivity had taught them to moan and sadly their deliverance had not automatically freed them from complaining. Unfortunately, these traits can be found in God's church today.

We are not devoid of grumpy people. Paul encountered the same in the early church. He wrote to the Philippians to do all things without murmuring and complaining. They should work out their salvation with fear and trembling knowing that God was at work in them to will and to do his good pleasure. The outcome would be that they would shine as lights in the world (Phil. 2:15). Murmuring and complaining often characterize our modern world. Simply to refuse that prevailing lifestyle and instead to express gratitude and appreciation will result in believers standing out in the workplace, the shops, schools, even restaurants. I recall a waiter who had been serving my co-elders and me who apologetically asked if he might interrupt our meal and say a word, 'I just want to say what a pleasure it is to serve you gentlemen.' There was no explanation, but we later presumed that maybe the treatment he had received at other tables was such that he had noted a difference with us. We had simply been appreciative and friendly. It was enough for him to take note. We hardly regarded ourselves as shining lights, but who knows how he was being treated elsewhere? God wants us to overflow with thanksgiving so that it simply becomes natural to us. Harsh language can kill your testimony in a moment. We need to speak in a way that people want to listen, and listen in a way that encourages people to speak.

In spite of their ingratitude, God once again overflowed in kindness towards them, providing a meal miraculously and not just once, but daily throughout their long wanderings. We are told in Deuteronomy 1:2–3 that the intended journey from Sinai to the Promised Land was eleven brief days, but because of their unbelief at Kadesh Barnea they circled the wilderness for forty years! Nevertheless, God continued providing manna to his unresponsive people daily throughout that extended journey.

Although the manna was a free gift from God and in no way a reward for their good behaviour, a pattern of discipline was imposed.

They were to collect and eat the manna on a daily basis, not hoard it, but to trust that on the next day it would miraculously appear again. Also, on the sixth day they were to gather enough for two days, so that they might rest on the sabbath. Embracing discipline was part of their growth programme, but sadly waywardness still prevailed. Obedience was yet to be learned. God had freely promised to provide on a daily basis, which was an expression of His kind favour towards them, but He wanted them to grow and begin to take responsible steps. He wanted them to leave the immaturity of slavery behind them and begin to learn obedience and prove themselves trustworthy. So with us. God's grace towards us is unending and unfathomable, but He wants us to grow in maturity. It has been said that many think that maturity comes with age, but no, growing old comes with age. Maturity comes with taking responsibility! I have known some impressively mature young people and sadly a number of very immature old people.

God's plan was to take a former slave community and prepare them for inheritance and make them a light to the nations. As slaves they had never owned anything, made choices or cultivated discretion. They had only known hard labour and whips. Soon they would inherit land and property and need to develop judgement and discrimination, make choices and progress towards management skills and become a mature people. Though some were learning, they could hardly be regarded as a disciplined nation.

Discipline without legalism

We too must learn to appreciate discipline, but distinguish it from legalism, which is where so many become confused. Some Christians feel that they have to somehow earn God's gifts by their personal conduct, almost fearing that, as it were, the manna would not appear if they did not show themselves worthy. No. The manna was God's gracious gift. God would supply it every day for years. So it is with God's grace to us. We can never earn His grace or show ourselves worthy. Because of Jesus and what he has accomplished for us, we can always expect God's gracious gifts to us, unearned and unmerited.

Grace has simply to be received. We are not required to impress God in order to receive grace. Jesus has already impressed God by His breathtaking obedience and sacrifice and we are accepted in him. We are hidden in the righteousness of the one who impressed God on our behalf. Yet being fully qualified for God's gifts does not mean we are simply to discard discipline that will help us grow in maturity. Jesus is my freely given righteousness, given once for all, but he is also happy to provide me with daily nourishment. He can be my daily manna. He freely offers himself as the true bread which comes down from heaven (John 6:33). You need to be regularly nourished by communion with him, celebrating His love, being sustained by the life which he imparts. If you never develop the discipline of coming to eat of him, fellowship with him, become increasingly consciously joined to Him you will frustrate His purpose.

God's intention was to transform a rabble of slaves into a disciplined army that could conquer and inherit the Promised Land. Lessons had to be learned. Strength had to be gained. Training had to be embraced. Nourishment was needed in order to make them the people he planned for them to become.

God will daily and freely supply us with grace and we can come and eat without money and without price (see Isaiah 55:1). He also wants us to learn to walk worthy of His indescribable grace in redeeming us from bondage and demonstrate ourselves to be His redeemed people in the midst of all the confusion that marks these end times.

14

If anyone thirsts

Water from the Rock. Exodus 17:1–7

As the deer pants for the water brooks, so my soul pants for you O God (Psalm 42:1).

Thirst is often used metaphorically in the Bible to represent human longings. Jesus once cried out in Jerusalem at a crowded feast day, 'If any one is thirsty let him come to me and drink' (John 7:37). He spoke to a five-times married woman about water he could supply that would not only satisfy her craving so that she would never thirst again, but would prove to be living water springing up to eternal life (John 4:14). The ultimate fulfilment of this biblical picture is finally expressed in the book of Revelation, 'They will no longer thirst any more' (Rev. 7:16).

We should not be surprised, therefore, to find that, as Israel progressed, the urgent necessity for drinking water surfaced. As we have seen, these things happened to them as an example and were written down for our instruction, and Paul says in the same passage that they all drank from the spiritual rock which followed them and the rock was Christ (1 Cor. 10:4).

But I'm getting ahead of myself.

We must return to Israel's journey. A huge dilemma confronted Israel. Where do you find water in a desert? The answer is that it was provided supernaturally. The Bible is not just a record of journey, it is littered with spectacular supernatural phenomena.

It is, after all, a book about the living God and His interaction with people. Once again, the Israelites directed their complaints to Moses. He became the butt of their hostility. Those called to lead God's people will often feel the heat. If they have not been called and commissioned by God, they will not stand the pressure. Volunteering to lead might appear noble, yet leadership skill is required which does not come from human temperament, but from the certain knowledge that almighty God has called and commissioned, you are His servant and there is nowhere else to go.

Moses was told to take the staff that God had owned so significantly throughout the plagues and at the Red Sea and strike the rock having God's promise that, when struck, it would supply water. The phenomenal nature of this miracle will be appreciated when you consider that Israel numbered two million people plus livestock. That represented a lot of thirst! Psalm 78:15–16 provides a vivid commentary: 'He split the rocks in the wilderness and gave them abundant drink like ocean depths. He brought forth streams also from the rock and caused waters to run down like rivers.' What flowed from the rock satisfied the two million and led to the psalmist using words like 'streams, rivers and even ocean depths', an awesome supply.

Paul interprets and makes spiritual application of this phenomenal overflow of water by telling us that the rock they drank from was 'a spiritual rock and that rock was Christ' (1 Cor. 10:4). He wanted us who live 'at the ends of the ages' (1 Cor. 10:11) to know that more than we could ever imagine is available in Christ. Christ's invitation was to anyone who was thirsty to come to him. He would not only never thirst again, but from his own innermost being would flow rivers of living water (John 7:18). Jesus unashamedly called thirsty people to have their needs more than adequately met in him. The conversation with the Samaritan woman that he encountered at a well, recorded in John 4, tells a vivid picture. She had been married five times and the man she was now with was not her husband. Obviously, she had led a tumultuous life, maybe repeatedly searching, hoping and failing to find what she longed for. Attractive enough for five men to want to marry her, now perhaps beginning to fade. The man now with her not bothering to officially tie the knot. She came at the middle of the day whereas most women would fetch their water early before the sun began to blaze. Maybe friendless, perhaps with a reputation.

A well on the inside

Jesus offered this woman not only living water, but water that would become in her a well of water springing up to eternal life. He offered her not simply a drink, but the well inside her. In this apparently confusing situation, she somehow realized that what was being offered would more than supply her need. She would no longer be thirsty nor have to come any longer to this well to draw. He was offering something that would supernaturally not only quench her thirst, but actually well up within. Sadly, many Christians seem to have failed to see what Jesus was offering. So many embrace the concept that what they need is outside of them and they need to keep coming to find it, but Jesus was promising her something within. That meant that she could throw away her bucket. She could have a well of living water springing up inside her. She herself could have rivers flowing from her innermost being. Jesus was offering something that would thoroughly satisfy. In John 7 we are told that, 'This he spoke of the Holy Spirit who those who believed in him were to receive', and we are told that when the Comforter comes he will abide or remain with us, supplying our deepest need, thoroughly quenching our thirst.

Even in times of outward testing and maybe tribulation, we are told that, 'tribulation produces character and that character produces perseverance and that perseverance produces hope which doesn't disappoint because the love of God is poured out in our hearts by the Holy Spirit' (Rom. 5:3–5), described by Douglas Moo in his commentary as an 'abundant, extravagant effusion'.

Paul insists that Christ was the rock which followed them. Moses had to strike the rock so that the water might flow. Paul didn't develop the theme, but we know that Christ our rock was terribly struck. He was wounded for our transgressions and crushed for our iniquities. By his scourging we are healed. The water that satisfies our thirst came from one who suffered in our place. When he cried from the Cross, 'I thirst', he thoroughly identified with us in our human vulnerability and all our cravings, and carried away our guilt.

Jesus can genuinely satisfy human thirst. New Christians need to be persuaded that this is so. This was a huge struggle for me as a young Christian. For some years I had been experiencing life with a close-knit group of manifestly non-Christian friends, and greatly feared that if I was to completely abandon the lifestyle that we enjoyed together and fully identify with Christ and his church, I would never find personal satisfaction. Having ultimately made my decision and cut my ties, I remember my first weekend. In those days we acknowledged that we endured every weekday and lived for the weekends. My home town of Brighton came alive at weekends with young people crowding the streets and the bars. I loved it and was captivated by the buzz of it all. My parents were not Christians and so far I had no Christian friends.

Having determined to leave my old lifestyle and thoroughly identify with Christ and his church, I started heading out on my wilderness journey. My first Saturday evening came around, so I took my motor scooter out and drove down town among the crowds, looked around, felt the tug, but determined to take my fresh stand. I drove home to our quiet end of town, put my bike away and sat indoors, on a Saturday night! My parents were in another room and I sat alone. So, this is Christianity! Sitting at home on a Saturday night alone. I was appalled. I was so empty. Would I be able to keep up Christianity? I feared I would die of thirst. Eventually I picked up my Bible and read through much of the book of Acts, something I had never done before. As I tasted the flavour of the early church and the explosive pace of its life, a bubble of hope stirred in my heart. Perhaps Christ could satisfy. Perhaps I would find something for my thirsty soul. And I did!

15

Amalek

Attacked without warning! Exodus 17:1–16

With no warning at all, suddenly the Israelites were attacked by a foreign army. No sign of a growing threat or the possibility of impending danger, but the Amalekites were upon them. Israel's very existence was threatened.

It needs to be understood that unexpected battles are part of the Christian life. Jesus and his apostles never promised us that the Christian walk would be trouble-free. Rather the opposite, Jesus spoke plainly that in the world we would have pressure and Paul later added that through much tribulation we enter the kingdom. Unsought battles will be encountered. Peter warned his readers not to be surprised at the fiery trial as though some strange thing were happening to them. They are to be regarded as par for the course.

Although Israel looked as though they were completely unprepared for warfare, they were actually going to learn a great deal through this whole episode. Unlike the conflict with Egypt and its army where they simply had to stand still and see the salvation of God and then walk freely through the Red Sea, now they must actually fight and play their own part. Israel's role was not to be passive as at the Red Sea, but far more active. Many battles were ahead. This first one would be very instructive.

A leader was appointed. We are introduced to Joshua and Joshua is introduced to warfare. Supposedly he had already been observed as a potential leader and fighter. He was told to select men. Actual fighting was to be involved; swords would be drawn, but soon it would become clear that they were no ordinary army. Human strength would be overshadowed by God's oversight and powerful participation. Some have interpreted the Red Sea crossing as a demonstration that God will only ever require believers to stand still and let Him fight all their battles. The phrase that we should simply 'let go and let God' has become popular in some circles. All we need to do is stand back and see what God will do. Yet this conflict will teach us other important lessons.

Joshua and his select army must fight and so must we. Paul urges us in Ephesians 6 not only to be strong, but to put on armour, anticipating a fight. The Old Testament is full of actual battles and the New Testament consistently uses battle language, calling us to be good soldiers. We are constantly reminded to be alert in the battle. So many Bible heroes are fighters, such as Joshua, Gideon and David, rather than philosophers, such as Socrates, Aristotle or Plato. Even Nehemiah, whose calling was to build a city, found he could not turn his back on the reality of battle. If you want to build something for God you will find opposition. You will have to learn to fight. Nehemiah and his men needed not only trowels with which to build, but swords for the conflict.

With all those practical preparations in mind, this proved to be extraordinary warfare. Moses climbed above the battle not to get a good view of what was taking place, but for a very different purpose. We soon discover that actually the outcome did not ultimately lie with Joshua's fighting skill, but in another force altogether. Moses, we are told, held up what had now come to be called 'the staff of God' in his hand (Exod. 17:9). It seems that what was formerly Moses' staff had become God's staff. Moses' hands were raised to

God holding the staff, which somehow signified and represented the covenant relationship God had established with Moses and the people. He had made them promises. He would stand by them, see them through and bring them into the promised land. Yet now their very existence was in jeopardy.

Hands raised in prayer

It was time to enlist His aid, call upon Him for His intervention and the release of His power. As Moses raised the staff in his hands, it was as though he was reminding God of His promises. When he did, God responded and Joshua's army in the valley prevailed. However, Moses grew weary. His arms began to sag, and as they did Amalek began to prevail again. Joshua, presumably with the same physical strength and battle skills, frustratingly found himself being driven back. He was fighting for all he was worth, but discovered that actually his military prowess was not dictating the outcome of the campaign. Success or failure in the fight were directly related to the degree to which Moses could keep his hands raised. His holding up of the staff held the key. Aaron and Hur came to Moses' aid. His hands were sustained and the battle was secured.

We in today's church must learn the crucial place of prevailing prayer in our conflicts. We must learn to hold up to God the promises He has made. Prayer is not trying to impose our plans on God, but becoming acquainted with His covenant promises, believing them, going in to battle because of them and then wholeheartedly reminding God of His commitment and our expectation that He will accomplish what only He can.

We send our best warriors into the battle, but then we pray. We actually fight the battle in prayer as though that is where the action really takes place. Sometimes this story needs to be translated into twenty-first century experience as we find ourselves in conflict situations. My home church in Brighton had outgrown its premises. We needed a larger location and discovered an ideal redundant warehouse in the centre of town. An informal enquiry to the Town Council led us to believe that an approach would be received favourably. As a church we raised a large offering and submitted our offer. To our amazement, it was categorically and dismissively rejected by the Council. We had been misled. They were not likely to allow good industrial property at the centre of town to become a church building! We asked if we could appeal against their decision, but were told it would be a waste of time since the Council's decision was a 100 per cent refusal judgement. We were told that had it been more balanced, such as 60:40 per cent, it might be worth appealing but one of 70:30 per cent or 80:20 per cent would fall on deaf ears. A 100 per cent decision certainly was not worth contesting.

Nevertheless, we sent our Joshua into the valley. Yes, we prepared the best possible argued appeal and sent it in. And then we fought in prayer. Our hands were raised to God fervently appealing to a higher authority, bringing to him His great promises to those who pray and believe. Repeated prayer meetings filled the weeks as we waited for the response. When it came, the 100 per cent refusal was thoroughly overturned. We won our battle. We not only gained our warehouse, we experienced the God who can win battles and overturn apparently impossible situations.

We read of the early church that they devoted themselves to prayer. Prisons were opened and men walked free. In the face of a hostile Sanhedrin the unlearned and untrained disciples instinctively lifted their voice to God. They saw Him as the sovereign Lord, the one able to fight their battles for them. Their opposition was powerful. No authority was higher than the Sanhedrin. The High Priest and his family together represented a formidable opposition, especially to these fishermen and others from the rural north. This was the big city and these men expected to be obeyed. The disciples were outwardly outclassed. However, they knew of another authority. They pressed their case to one who had created the heavens and the earth and was himself Lord with all authority in heaven and earth.

Like Moses, they raised their hands to a higher power. Refusing to back down they cried to God for the requisite boldness and power to advance their battle, preach the gospel and extend Christ's kingdom. Great power was unleashed. The very building shook. Filled again with the Holy Spirit, they pressed forward. Fear was defeated and the enemy could not withstand them. The same Sovereign Lord who was accessible to Moses was there for the Apostles and can be sought by us today. His power is as it always was. If we are to advance with the gospel, we need to rediscover and take advantage of the power of prayer and prove the faithfulness of our mighty God.

16

Jethro's advice

Humility and change. Exodus 18

When I first encountered this chapter as a young pastor it had a very significant impact on the formation of our young church. It led to quite a transformation in the way that we 'did' church.

Thus far in our story, the Israelites are a nation on the move with no particular structure or shape, a vast conglomeration of former slaves who had yet to be transformed into a nation, a society with its own distinct culture. God's ultimate goal was for a holy people, one for His own possession out of all the peoples on the face of the earth (Deut. 7:6). They were to be a light to the nations.

A fascinating encounter took place which led to a key breakthrough. Jethro, Moses' father-in-law, came to meet him. Amazed at their escape, 'he rejoiced over all the goodness which Yahweh had done to Israel in delivering them from the hand of the Egyptians' (Exod. 18:9). Overwhelmed and astounded at the power of Israel's God, he too became a believer and offered sacrifices. The following day he witnessed how Israel were coping on their journey. Moses was besieged by a never-ending line of people queuing up to bring their questions to him for judgement. Plainly this was a recipe for disaster, a completely unsustainable mode of operation, so Jethro offered his advice.

One of the first things we can learn from this story is how Moses' personal humility made the way possible for key transition.

Why should the mighty Moses, who had confronted Pharaoh and whose staff opened the Red Sea, take any notice of this recent convert? Wasn't he God's man, following God's instructions? If God wanted to change things. surely he could have spoken directly to Moses about it. Thankfully Moses didn't adopt that stance, but was open to listen.

Humility in leadership is crucial in God's kingdom. Tragically in recent years the church has witnessed the demise of a number of very high-profile leaders. Prominent names have disappeared from the limelight and more than once the reason for their removal has been the inappropriate use of leadership power and authority. They had become unassailable in their position of supremacy. As 'the Lord's anointed' they had assumed inappropriate attitudes, making them beyond question. Becoming increasingly lonely and isolated, they lost the plot, lost their people and several have lost their jobs. Happily Moses, later described as the meekest man on earth, didn't adopt that stance (Num. 12:3). His willingness to be confronted opened the door to progress.

Jethro did not approach him as a time and motion expert projecting his worldly knowhow. Overwhelmed at God's powerful intervention at the Red Sea, he had become a true believer, but he had not been crushed from years of slavery and could see how ineffective was Moses' isolated leadership. It was obvious to him that not only was Moses on course for self-destruction, but that the people would also eventually grow exhausted from their quaint way of working. Jethro offered some excellent counsel.

First, he helped define Moses' own role, pointing out the things that he uniquely could do. He should be the people's representative before God. His first responsibility was to be a man of prayer. As the story unfolds, his extraordinary courage and authority in prayer played a massive role in their progress, even to the point of his standing alone between God's holy wrath and the danger of their being obliterated. As we shall later see, his stunning role as an intercessor literally saved them.

Surely the prime calling of every Christian leader must be to pray for those they serve. Jesus modelled this, as did Paul, labouring ceaselessly for the churches he had planted. We shall look in more detail at Moses' extraordinary example in prayer later in our story.

Second, he was to be their teacher. They would need his instruction in two particular ways. First, he was to teach the statutes and laws, the unchangeable truths that God would soon reveal at Mount Sinai. God's holy law would be given to Moses and he was to carefully communicate that law to the people. They were going to be a distinctive people who could boast that no other nation had such holy laws as they. Moses was uniquely qualified and called to receive these laws from God and present them to the nation, something only he was appointed to do. Secondly, having established God's great objective law, he was to teach the people how to walk and what they must do. The law would teach them their identity in relationship with God and from that identity should flow a lifestyle. This pattern should be found in the local church where leaders should instruct their people regarding the great truths of Christ and the salvation which he has imparted, creating a new people in Christ. Secondly, they should instruct in the lifestyle appropriate for such a people. The epistles of the New Testament, perhaps notably Paul's epistles, follow this pattern of declaring great gospel truth and then urging appropriate lifestyle, calling his people to walk worthy of the truth which they have embraced. As Christians we are not on a mystical search for God.

He has spoken wonderful truths, flowing out from the salvation that Jesus has obtained changing us from slaves into sons of God. When we receive this powerful truth, it sets us free. Nevertheless, we need guidance to know how to walk in order to please God.

Having established his unique role, Moses was also to select able men who feared God, men of truth who hate dishonest gain, and place them as leaders of thousands, hundreds, fifties, and tens. They were to judge the people in minor disputes so that only major disputes should be brought to Moses. When I first became a Christian, I was so grateful for the excellent pastor in the church which I joined, who was such a fine and beloved Bible teacher, but it was quite a large congregation which made it very difficult to feel part of a family, gain friendships and to get beyond knowing anybody apart from formal greetings at the church door on Sunday mornings. When later I became a pastor, it was through confronting this chapter of Jethro's advice which led me to introduce a small group structure in the church. In those days it was regarded as a radical step, but proved a huge blessing to the church. More people were taking responsibility as group leaders and people began to find one another in a far more intimate way, creating a context for leadership development and a wider group of people taking responsibility in church life.

Sharing leadership

Leaders must learn this crucial lesson in our modern church. There are many responsibilities that can be shared with others. Qualified people will happily fulfil many roles in church life, resulting in many discovering their own particular gifts and opportunities to serve. The New Testament paints the picture of a many-membered body with each employing their specific gift in serving others and building up the body of Christ. A local church was never meant to be built on one prominent or exclusive gift. The whole body will be far stronger when each member is working properly and many are released to serve and find their place in the body.

Jethro's advice was embraced and a formless mass of ex-slaves began to take on a new shape. Leaders at various levels began to emerge. Instead of everybody waiting in line for the opportunity to speak to Moses, help became far more accessible. Moses was given clear instruction regarding the type of leaders that God wanted, namely men of ability and character, both crucial for the security of the flock. Ability is, of course, essential, but character seems to outweigh ability in Jethro's instruction. A similar emphasis will be found in the New Testament, where qualifications for elders and deacons are heavily weighted towards the need of godly character.

Though Moses was so evidently their ultimate leader, the appointment of other leaders was a significant development in their becoming a nation gradually taking shape. So, in the New Testament Paul would evangelize in virgin territory, lead a number to Christ and form a community, but the appointment of godly church elders was a vital factor in forming a new local church. Each new church needed a team of mature, God-appointed elders for his foundation-laying work as an apostle to be fulfilled. As a wise master builder, he knew the keys to laying a good foundation, part of which was the establishing of elders in leadership positions.

Jethro's intervention in their progress as a nation played a key role in the possibility of their ongoing success on the journey. Having made his contribution, however, he did not assume authority or provide ultimate guidance. They continued following the cloud of God's presence.

17

God's treasured possession carried on eagles' wings

God speaks! Exodus 19

One side of a tapestry shows all the knots and loose ends of the thread; the other a beautiful picture. Now we are allowed to see the developing story from God's perspective. We have been looking at all the bumps in the road, the questionings, complaints, battles and breakthroughs. Now God told Moses what he had been observing, breathtaking in its beauty. He saw a special treasure of a nation not simply fleeing from Egypt through a wilderness, but being brought to himself, carried on eagles' wings.

God's view of His own people is always so surprising, tender and loving. They are His own possession of all the peoples of the earth (see Exod. 19:5). He reminded them, 'You have seen what I did to the Egyptians. I thoroughly destroyed your enemy and ended your bondage, changed your status from slaves to free men', and something far more wonderful, 'out of Egypt I called my son' (Hos. 11:1). Later Moses, singing his prophetic song, reflected more on this image declaring, 'The Lord's portion is His people... he found him in a desert land, the howling waste of a wilderness; he circled him, he cared for him, he guarded him as the apple of His eye. Like an eagle that stirs up its nest, that hovers over its young, he spread His wings and caught them and carried them on His pinions' (Deut. 32:10–11). God saw them as a young eagle uniquely cared for by him, His majestic wingspan covering their every need. He brought them not simply to a mountain called Sinai, but far more intimately, 'I brought you to myself'. Even though their physical destination was Canaan their ultimate destination was the Lord himself. On planet earth, where mankind had been barred from knowing God, East of Eden, excluded from the tree of life, condemned to death, there was a special nation in process of being brought not only out of Egypt, but out of death to God himself. God's plan of worldwide redemption was beginning to unfold initially in this unique nation.

Out of Egypt He had called His son, birthed out of the waters of the Red Sea, like a new creation. So tenderly He recorded, 'It is I who taught Ephraim to walk. I took them in my arms, but they didn't know I healed them. I led them with the cords of human-kindness, with the bands of love and I became as one who eases the yoke on their jaws and bent down to feed them' (Hos. 11:4). So intimate, so personal and sounding so like the Lord Jesus when he invited the lost and weary not to come to religion, but to come to himself and learn from his meek and lowly heart and find rest for their souls. God was bringing a lost people home to himself.

If we follow the story and fix our gaze on the messy side of the tapestry with all of Israel's obvious failures and misdemeanours we should be amazed at God's awesome perspective. Later we will meet Balaam, a kind of renegade prophet, who was hired by an enemy nation to curse Israel, but found he couldn't. Instead he uttered some of the most sublime prophesies about God's blessing on His covenant people and described them in extraordinarily glowing terms.

'There is no omen against Jacob, God sees no trouble in Israel.

The Lord his God is with him and the shout of the king is among them' (Num. 23:21). They were a redeemed people who had sheltered under the blood of the Passover lamb. Guilt had been covered, a lamb had died. Soon they would be instructed to build a tabernacle where offerings could continually be brought and a regular day of atonement established. Guilt would be thoroughly removed from the camp.

God's unique nation

They would be a unique people who, unlike any other nation on earth would experience the actual presence of God with them. They were to be a kingdom of priests and a holy nation, knowing God and representing Him to the world (Exod. 19:6). Here was Israel's mission statement, defining their purpose as God's people. Enigmatically made holy by their unique relationship with God as his special treasure, but also called to be holy because of this same relationship.

Later God would again express His special delight in Israel as chosen to be a people for His own possession out of all the peoples on the face of the earth, adding that he didn't set His love on them or choose them because they were more in number than any of the peoples, for they were the fewest, but because the Lord loved them (see Deut. 7:6–8). The mystery of God's electing love expressed here so tenderly would repeatedly be referred to and be given as the reason for them to be exclusively different to other nations, reflecting the privilege of that relationship. They were not only His possession, but His *treasured* possession with exclusive access to His heart so that they might uniquely make him known as a kingdom of priests and a holy nation. Yahweh remained God of the whole world yet was in special relationship with Israel, not as an end itself, but ultimately for the sake of the nations.

Peter unashamedly took this language to describing Israel's relationship with God and applied it to Christ's church. Now 'We are His chosen race and royal priesthood, holy nation and a people for God's own possession so that we may proclaim the excellencies of him who called us out of darkness into His marvellous light' (1 Pet. 2:9).

Once we were not a people, but now we are God's people.

As believers in Christ we are now invited to take the language of such affection and personal delight to ourselves. Tragically, Christ's contemporaries, those originally given the promises, stumbled over and rejected the rock of offence who became the very cornerstone of a new living temple. Now Peter tells us we are to live as aliens and strangers, not participating in the world's ungodly style. Our experience is like Israel's. Having been delivered from slavery and given the gift of righteousness and enjoying His love and acceptance, we are to live a completely different lifestyle. We don't do this trying to achieve our salvation or approval, but because it has been given to us freely by the grace of God.

For Israel, they were brought collectively as a nation, for us we are brought individually through the gospel to our own personal experience of His acceptance and delight. We who were once far off have been brought near and now inherit the glorious privileges that are ours in Christ. We too can look at the other side of the tapestry, seeing the church from God's eyes, holy and blameless before him, the delight of His heart.

18

Meeting God!

God's holy loyalty. Exodus 20 (and 21–31!)

'Moses brought the people to meet God' (Exod. 19:17). What an extraordinary statement. I remember as a young student being brought by my fiancée to meet her parents. I was a little nervous. What should I wear? What would I say? How should I address them? It was quite an occasion. Moses brought the people to meet God!

They had met Moses and even learned to follow the cloud and seen extraordinary signs and wonders in Egypt and the Red Sea open, but now to meet God! We are told that they stood at the foot of Mount Sinai, which was suddenly covered in smoke because the Lord descended on it in fire and the great mountain quaked violently. God had come to the meeting. Then a trumpet sound which grew louder and louder. Moses spoke. The answer was a terrifying crash of thunder. The Lord came down on the top of Mount Sinai. Thunder, lightening and the piercing trumpet sound left the people terrified, forbidden even to touch the mountain. They pleaded with Moses to speak for them on God's behalf, fearing that if God addressed them directly they would die. The prospect of hearing the naked voice of God filled them with dread beyond the sound of crashing thunder.

Earlier for Moses a single bush had blazed with heavenly glory. Moses had quickly removed his sandals since the very ground had become holy. Now, for the nation, the whole mountain became incandescent. Now the nation of two million were having their encounter with God's magnificent holiness, glory and power. Beyond the fire and brightness came God's own voice declaring His identity as the Lord their God who had brought them out of Egyptian slavery, His favourite way of referring to himself.

Now He was establishing His holy covenant with them. They were to have no other gods. He was a jealous God whose very name was Jealous, fervently and passionately committed to His betrothed. No other suitors were to be countenanced. He wanted their undivided devotion. This fierce jealousy must not be misunderstood. We tend to regard jealousy as an ugly trait, associating it with suspicion, mistrust, envy, negativity, always misreading situations and leaping to false conclusions. God has no illusions. Suspicion is foreign to Him since He knows everything. God's jealousy therefore must be understood as the purest of loves, expressing the utter horror that any loving husband would feel at the thought of sharing his wife with another. Israel was His special treasure, loved by Him with an everlasting love (Jer. 31:3). This was not fundamentally about rule keeping, but loyalty. He is not a fastidious deity with an itemised check list, but a loving, jealous God looking for love and loyalty from those He had lovingly redeemed. Our story makes it clear that the land was given to a people whom the Lord had already redeemed. The ten commandments were never meant to be a means of earning favour, still less a way of being redeemed. They were given to a people whom Yahweh had already brought out of slavery.

From now on they were to be His covenant people, so they would obviously need to embrace an appropriate lifestyle. He was holy so they would obviously need to be holy. What follows constitutes God's law, the Torah. It needs to be understood as simply reflecting God's own holiness and actually, if lived out, the recipe for a community's fulfilment and joy, keeping them from sin and sadness. Any people embracing these wondrous values would rightly honour God, not be misled into foolishness of following dumb idols, celebrate a regular day of rest, have a healthy, secure family life, never murder, commit adultery, steal or lie, and be content with what they owned, free from coveting. What a great society! Wouldn't the world be a better place if we all embraced these glorious values?

Sadly, our New Testament explains to us that the law itself could never produce the lifestyle that God wanted. The law was holy, faultless and good, but it was weakened by human flesh (Rom. 8:4). The law could only describe, and indeed command, the appropriate conduct for God's people. It could not actually accomplish or produce it. Paul told the Galatians that if a law had been given which was able to impart life, then righteousness would have been based on law (Gal. 3:21). Sadly, the commandment which was meant to result in life proved to result in death (Rom. 7:10). It made God's holy requirements very clear and brought sharp distinction between light and darkness, but Israel's fallen nature could not rise to the challenge. The law became a heavy burden and the very thing that ultimately condemned them. Sinai, which featured initially as a place of covenant betrothal between God and His elect bride, was later regarded as a place of slavery and tyranny (Gal. 5:25), especially when contrasted with the wonder of the New Covenant sealed by Christ's blood.

We come to Mount Zion

The book of Hebrews reveals that the church has not come to a mountain which cannot be touched and to a blazing fire... to the blast of a trumpet and the sound of words that those hearing begged that no more should be spoken to them, the mountain which could not be touched for fear of being stoned, but in stark contrast has come to Mount Zion, the city of the Living God, the heavenly Jerusalem, and ultimately to Jesus, the mediator of a New Covenant (see Hebrews 12:18–24). What a privilege we New Covenant believers have! We come not to Sinai but to Jesus. The prohibition not to even touch the mountain is replaced by the gentle invitation actually to come to him, the God who came in the flesh, and this with the added revelation that He is gentle and lowly in heart. No wonder the writer to the Hebrews celebrates that this is a better covenant! (Heb. 8:6). Jesus does not come with the heavy yoke of the law, but with an easy yoke, a light burden and a promise that we can learn from Him and find rest for our souls. What a contrast!

We are now Christ's bride in a covenant of grace, discharged from the old covenant which Christ himself fulfilled, and not under law but under grace (Rom. 6:14).

Now the spirit of life in Christ Jesus has set us free from the law of sin and death as our master but at the same time enabling us to fulfil the law's requirement by our walking no more in the flesh, but in the Spirit (Rom. 8:2–4). If we embrace the Holy Spirit's life within, we will find that the life we live will accomplish God's desire. The man under the law might say that he desires to do God's will, but lacks the ability. He may 'will' but he cannot 'do' (Rom. 7:18). Yet Paul now has better news for us that God is at work in us both to 'will' and to 'do' God's will (Phil. 2:13). In Christ and by his Spirit, the New Covenant provides both the willing and the power to do.

The gospel also invites us to come and meet God but, praise God, the invitation comes with such tenderness from the one who satisfied the law's demands on our behalf and provides us with his own righteousness, so that we can find rest. Being justified by faith we have peace with God (Rom. 5:1), 'For Christ also died for sins once for all, the just for the unjust so that he might bring us to God' (1 Pet. 3:18). Moses brought the people to meet God. How much better is the New Covenant where Jesus, our much better mediator, has truly brought us to God.

19

The golden calf

Meanwhile, down the mountain… Exodus 32

How fickle can you get? Moses was on Sinai's heights in God's presence, but in the valley the people quickly grew weary of waiting for him. Just a few weeks earlier, trembling from the sight and voice of God, the Israelites had promised their loyalty; 'All that the Lord has spoken we will do' (Exod. 24:7). Blood was sprinkled, covenant was established. Then after such a brief delay their loyalty was shown to be like a morning cloud. Complaining that they didn't know what had become of Moses, they urged Aaron to manufacture a god of their own specifications who would go before them.

Gold jewellery, recently taken as spoil from the Egyptians, was brought to Aaron and he fashioned a golden calf. How quickly he yielded to their pressure and proved such a frail leader simply responding to their demands. His ineffective leadership stood in stark contrast to what Moses provided as a mediator in the crisis that followed.

The all-seeing God was fully aware of the chaos breaking out below. Aaron gave credit to a golden calf that he had just made for masterminding the exodus from Egypt, following which they offered burnt offerings and peace offerings and so repudiated their unique relationship with God. Moses' role as mediator was never more evident than in what followed. In response to Israel's choosing another man-made god, God appeared to disown Israel, referring to them as '*your people* whom *you* brought out from Egypt', adding, 'I've seen *this people* and they are an obstinate people' (Exod. 32:7–9). Moses, however, would have none of this and quickly responded, 'O Lord, why does your anger burn against *your* people whom *you* have brought out from Egypt with great power and a mighty hand?'

Moses was quick to resist the implication that the nation was his responsibility. They were *God's* people. God's power had secured their deliverance. God had publicly bound himself to them through His mighty deliverance from Egypt. Perhaps the most stunning words in the whole encounter are God's words to Moses, 'Let me alone that my anger may burn against them and I might destroy them and I will make of you a great nation.' Here Moses was distinguished from the nation. God made him an amazing offer. He would destroy the nation and start again with Moses as the new Abraham, the new father of a people. As mediator, Moses stood between God and the people. He held no responsibility or guilt in connection with what had happened below, and was therefore in a unique context. God had made him an awesome offer, but the phrase 'let me alone' reveals that Moses immediately tried to withstand God in taking this course of action.

As an excellent mediator, he argued his case. What would the Egyptians say? They will claim that you brought the people out just to destroy them. His motivation was thoroughly God-centred. He was jealous for his reputation before Egypt and the nations. Secondly, he reminded God of his promises to Abraham, Isaac and Israel. He reminded God of his integrity as a God who keeps his word, and in using the name Israel rather than Jacob he underlined how God had especially bound himself to this people.

God's purpose to bless all the nations through their seed had been clearly stated. Failure to follow through with his promises would jeopardize his great international plan. His appeal was based completely on God's glory, reputation and ultimate plan, not on any excuse for Israel or appeal to consider their merit.

A true mediator

Later, Moses himself came down and saw their rebellion first-hand. Three thousand died as he called for an end to the rebellion and fresh dedication to God following their gross sin. Outraged by their idolatry, he shattered the tablets containing the ten commandments.

The following day he climbed the mountain again with another request, namely that God would forgive them, even offering to have his own name removed from God's book for their sake. As a true mediator, he fully identified with the law-giver and the law-breakers, profoundly jealous for God's glory, but also compassionately bound up with the people that he was leading. Although this request was denied, Moses' attempts to be an atoning mediator clearly point to one who will be like Moses and who will one day come (Deut. 18:18).

Thirdly, God offered a new arrangement. He would no longer be personally present on the journey, but would send an angel before them. He still spoke of their safe arrival in the Land (Exod. 33:2), but his personal presence would be withdrawn. Here Moses was absolutely insistent: 'If your presence doesn't go with us, don't lead us up from here.' He was not content to simply travel to the Land, enter it and enjoy its fruit. He passionately argued that it was the wondrous privilege of God being with them that made them a unique nation, distinct from all the nations on the face of the earth. What other people could make this breathtaking claim? His personal commitment to be their God, actually accessible among them, was central to God's whole purpose. This is what would make them a distinct people, a priestly kingdom and a holy nation. Moses' intercession prevailed. The promise of God's presence was renewed. Again, they could celebrate this distinction of God's presence among them. Moses' passionate and single-purposed intervention as a God-appointed mediator was fundamental to their actual survival and the fulfilment of God's original promise to Abraham that through his seed all the families of the earth would be blessed.

Before this episode is over, we see Moses once again invited by God to present himself at the top of Sinai, where God presented him with two fresh stones like the former ones, and the covenant was renewed. All this against the background of Moses' insatiable appetite to know God more fully. 'I pray you, show me your glory.' Moses was not content to simply represent God to the people and the people to God as a God-appointed go-between. As mediator for God, he longed to know him more intimately that he might more perfectly understand the person he represented. He had become a God-besotted man. The Lord responded with a promise that he would make all his goodness pass before him. The Lord then descended in a cloud and stood there with him and passed by him in front of him, proclaiming, 'The Lord, the Lord God, compassionate and gracious, slow to anger and abounding in loving kindness and truth.' He was given an extraordinary and phenomenal revelation of God's majesty and mercy.

Ultimately Moses came down from Sinai carrying the two replaced tablets, not knowing that his face shone, causing the people to tremble (Exod. 34:29). This would lead to frequent meetings with God and the repeated phenomenon of the shining face. As mediator, he entered into an awe-inspiring relationship with God, yet stood meek and lowly among the people and ultimately paid a heavy price for his full identification with them, pointing to one who would come as the ultimate mediator, fully God but fully man, displaying the Father's glory, but carrying away our shame.

20

Raising an offering

Giving to God's glory. Exodus 33.

As Israel travelled as a tent-dwelling people, God wanted His own tent among them. This tent would be fundamental to their experience of God's presence in the camp. Detailed instructions were given and the construction of the sanctuary was to be exactly as prescribed by God. This 'tent of meeting' would not simply appear like manna from the sky. They would have to construct it, and not only a tent but an altar, an ark and sundry other features, all to be gold-covered and encrusted with jewels which they would have to provide. So, we come to the first record of God's congregation bringing their gifts in worship to God. Again, instructive for us in so many ways.

Attitudes to money in the context of religion can become complicated. People can become suspicious, resentful, reluctant and even feel put upon or manipulated. Outsiders are particularly critical, complaining that churches just want your money. Some giving can be extraordinarily nominal, simply donating the left-overs. Other giving could only be described as profoundly sacrificial. Many diverse attitudes can be found in God's church.

Here, we see some vital principles for worshipping God in our giving.

Firstly, their giving was an act of worship which God himself asked for. It was His idea and essentially it was for Him, reflecting their unique relationship with Him. In that sense, it was to be their personal response to Him as their God. This should be fundamental in our attitude to offerings. This was not a 'whip round' or simply a collection.

It is evident that Jesus took the matter of money and giving very seriously, speaking often about it. Most pastors or church leaders tend to avert their gaze when people bring their offerings to church. Jesus didn't. He observed what people gave and made explicit comments about the amounts given and what the gifts represented, exonerating the gift of two coins that the poor widow gave against the larger, but flamboyant gift of the pharisee. Worship expressed by giving mattered to him. When a woman splashed perfume over him worth a year's salary, some expressed outrage at the waste, but he said her extravagant devotion would be referred to wherever the gospel was preached. She had come nearer to knowing and loving the one who came in order to give everything.

This brings us to the second observable feature, namely that God wanted everyone whose heart moved Him to raise the contribution (Exod. 25:2). It was to be heartfelt, not obligatory. When the offering actually took place, we are told that 'everyone whose heart stirred Him and everyone whose spirit moved him' came and brought their contribution (Exod. 25:21). Their giving was to represent worship from the heart. God had no appetite for forced or reluctant giving. He gave clear and detailed instructions how the manna was to be collected, but in contrast He wanted their giving to be heartfelt and spontaneous. Paul expressed a similar attitude. Regarding an offering that he hoped to receive from the Corinthians, He plainly stated, 'I am not speaking this as a command' (1 Cor. 8:8), adding, 'each one must do just as he has purposed in his heart, not grudgingly or under compulsion, for God loves a cheerful giver' (1 Cor. 9:7).

Surely reluctant worship is an oxymoron! Nevertheless, like them, we often need our spirits to move us. If their hearts were 'made willing' it implies that, left to themselves, they might have been indisposed. Of the early church it says, 'Great grace was on them all' and that grace released them to give. Paul, writing to the Corinthians to encourage their giving, told them of the grace of God given to the Macedonians, which freed them to contribute. Often, we need our natural caution or even fear to be overcome by grace from God so that our spirits become moved and freshly released to give. Then it becomes true heartfelt worship, not reluctant duty. Sometimes our human nature struggles with simple statements from Jesus, such as 'it is better to give than to receive'. We might think that receiving seems pretty enjoyable. We need faith to embrace his revelation and fresh stirrings of grace to lift our hearts to give generously. Sometimes, that can be quite literally a stirring, as I found on one occasion.

I remember leading my home church as we were approaching another particular gift day, wanting to raise in the region of £100,000. John Major as prime minister had introduced a saving plan called a TESSA, made attractive by being tax-free. As a responsible husband and father I had made a monthly investment over the required seven year program. Mine was about to mature. On the relevant Sunday we were gathered in worship and singing a song of devotion which began, "I will worship" in which the men and women sang with a responsive echo. The key verse was as follows:

> I will bow down,
> Hail you as king.
> I will serve you,
> Give you everything.[6]

As the women sang the response "Give you everything", I heard so clearly the Lord say in my heart, "Thank you, I'll have the TESSA". It was so tender and imparted fresh grace. The TESSA went into the offering.

God provided

God wanted a glorious tabernacle and they would have to construct and furnish it, but He ensured that they had what was necessary. It was He who told Abraham at the beginning that after 400 years of slavery they would leave Egypt with great possessions (Gen. 15:14). Moses gave them clear instructions that they were to plunder the Egyptians, asking their neighbours for gold, silver and clothing, which they readily gave. God asked them for their offerings, but He had first enabled and enriched them, making it possible for a slave community to give generously. The fact was that they could only give because God had provided them with the wherewithal to do so. They had been penniless slaves with no possessions, potential or dignity, but God had transformed everything. True worship is an acknowledgement of that reality. We can give because God has originally provided for us, not only materially but in every way. Gratitude for God's mercy and kindness in supplying our resources can transform our perspective.

Those who were made willing might also have excitedly grasped that their offering would henceforth become part of the actual tabernacle. 'My gold might help cover the ark, become part of the altar!' They might well have become stirred to participate because God's desire for a tabernacle began to thrill them and they could be tangibly involved. As a people they began to enter into the wonder of being caught up in this massive privilege.

They continued bringing freewill offerings every morning (Exod. 36:3). In the end, the cry was raised, 'No more!' More than enough had been offered (Exod. 36:7). Such a similar testimony could be found in the early church. The great grace that was on them transformed them to such a degree that they relinquished their exclusive right to their own possessions and shared wherever a need was apparent.

There were many sad and even dreadful days on Israel's journey, but this was a truly happy one when the people's hearts were so stirred to worship, and expressed that worship through giving their possessions. God is so worthy of our worship, but especially pleased when we delight to do His will. He hates reluctant externalism. The attitude of giving as little as we can get away with, or simply obeying a prescribed rule is so far removed from true worship.

Grace sets us free to respond to God, fills our hearts with gratitude, replaces our fears with confidence, thrills us with motivation to see God's habitation built. I have had the joy and privilege again and again to witness people made willing in the day of His power; I have frequently witnessed what seem to be amazing and ridiculous offerings, sometimes for the poor, other times to supply funds to buy buildings that have become meeting places for worship. God is still at work inviting worship expressed in giving and delighting in the response of His willing people.

21

The tabernacle

Where God dwells. Exodus 40

Following pages of detail, the tabernacle was completed and suddenly God was in the midst of His people in a fresh way. A tent so filled with God's presence that Moses could not enter (Exod. 40:34). The glory that had capped the mountain flooded the tent. The creator of the universe was now to be located particularly among the Israelites in this God-appointed location. The Bible is very clear that the omnipresent God fills His creation. There is nowhere where He is absent. Nevertheless, this tabernacle held a particular concentration of His presence and that so intense and recognizable that Moses could only observe at a distance. This stunning phenomenon demonstrated the glorious mystery of the unique privilege enjoyed by Israel. The tabernacle became a portable Sinai enshrining Yahweh's presence.

Their carefully appointed and consecrated priesthood would be able to enter God's holy place on their behalf, offer sacrifices, make atonement, receive mercy, provide a God-appointed ritual making it possible for God to remain in their midst and provide priestly blessing. He was present, dwelling among them as their God but, apart from Moses and the priests, still distant from the experience of the individual Israelite. So, the tabernacle signified both God's close proximity and His distance, His accessibility yet separateness. The glory of the Lord dwelt among them and Aaron and the priests mediated the blessing of His presence. When Moses and Aaron reappeared to bless the people the glory of the Lord appeared to all, fire fell to consume the offering and the people saw it, shouted and fell on their faces (Lev. 9:24). God was truly and manifestly among His people and His presence made them a unique nation on planet earth.

When the Apostle John wrote the prologue to his gospel, he clearly had the birth of the tabernacle in mind. Introducing the incarnation of Christ, he recorded, 'In the beginning was the word and the word was with God and the word was God' (John 1:1). No doubt filled with wonder he added, 'The word became flesh and dwelt (actually 'tabernacled') among us and we beheld His glory' (John 1:14). Tabernacle perspectives were clearly in mind. God who had always planned to be among them made this awesome commitment, no longer in a tent made with animal skins, but in human form.

In the New Testament God was now among His people in an unimagined way. Great is the mystery, the incarnate God veiled in flesh. God was actually walking among His people, eating with them, sharing life with them. Later John would write, 'The life was manifested. We have seen with our eyes, we've looked at and touched with our hands' (1 John 1:1–3). John actually rested and leaned on him yet he would say to Philip, 'He who has seen me has seen the Father' (John 14:9). He was the radiance of the Father's glory, like a sunbeam coming from the sun. We cannot look directly at the sun, but we can gaze on a sunbeam. Yet what is a sunbeam if it is not the radiance pouring down from the sun itself? So no man has seen God at any time, but this one who is in the bosom of the Father has made him known. God up close. God who can be known and touched and evidently with us, the exact image of the Father living among men. What God always had intended, God with us, tabernacling in a way that far exceeded a glory-filled tent.

While with them he revolutionized their lives. He took ordinary men, fishermen, tax collectors and the like and lived among them. Though he, and no doubt they, had nowhere to lay their heads, life was transformed. Nets were filled with fish, water turned into wine, terrifying storms hushed with a word, thousands fed with a tiny picnic, dead people called back to life, lame made to walk, blind made to see, deaf made to hear. Tenderness and compassion displayed in a completely unprecedented way. As for the words that came from His lips, no man ever spoke like this man. He opened His mouth and spoke and they were captivated. Each day spent in the presence of God seemed to surpass the previous day. Each waking morning filled them with anticipation.

He was leaving

Then on one momentous day, when they were totally unprepared, he spoke words they never anticipated or wanted to hear. 'I am with you a little while longer... where I am going you cannot come' (John 13:33). Who can imagine the terrible sense of loss? He had become their life. They had left everything to be with him. For them, being a disciple did not simply mean attending a church building each Sunday and maybe a mid-week meeting. It meant spending your life daily with Christ. The one full of glory who had been tabernacling among them was going to leave. How could we describe the consternation among them? The one who had transformed their whole experience of life was going away. The tabernacle was to be taken down, being a brief visit after all. They were going to be on their own again.

Then, no doubt crushed and shattered, they heard him say, 'I will not leave you as orphans, I will come to you' (John 14:18). What a rollercoaster! Oh, he's not leaving! He's coming back! He's just said it. He will not leave us orphans! I can imagine Peter wanting to reprimand Jesus and tell him never to frighten them again like that! To live without him was a devastating thought. How could they return to life as it had been before?!

Thank God the church was not going to be a group of people gathering to a fading memory of when God used to actually be among us, getting together trying to recall what it was like to actually be in His presence, trying hard to remember and record their sensational experience of actually living in close proximity to the living God, sadly now departed.

Before them was the horror of the Cross, the breathtaking discovery of the resurrection, the awesome sight of his ascension in a cloud to heaven, but on the Day of Pentecost suddenly from heaven fire fell, the temple was filled, the presence of God overwhelmed the new dwelling place of God. It had not been a fleeting visit! He was back! God's people could still own the glorious testimony of enjoying His presence. Now, like Moses, we can pray, 'If your presence does not go with us don't lead us up from here' (Exod. 33:15). Confronting the Sanhedrin and commanded no longer to preach Christ, the disciples cried to their sovereign Lord and, being filled once again with his holy presence, they pressed on with their calling to preach the gospel, filled with his power and boldness. God was manifestly among His people as the book of Acts makes very clear.

Later, Paul will teach that the church is a building fitted together and growing into a holy temple in the Lord in whom you also are being built together into a dwelling of God in the Spirit (Eph. 2:21–22). God's Spirit would actually dwell amongst us. Peter will add that we are as living stones being built up as a spiritual house (1 Pet. 2:5). God's intention to be among His people has never been rescinded. Believers must anticipate and welcome His wonderful presence, particularly when they gather in His name, eager to hear His word and worship him in celebration of the wonder of the living God being among them. Let us not settle for anything less.

22

Atonement for sin

The Holy-Love of God. Leviticus 16

The tabernacle certainly bore testimony to God's great desire to be among His people, but it also provided a context where sin and atonement were central issues. The recently-given law had made clear what was required and forbidden, and the tabernacle and its contents provided a setting where mercy could be provided through sacrifice and atonement. So, God was not only present, but through the tabernacle had provided a way for His people to draw near.

The word 'holiness' occurs thirty-seven times in Exodus in connection with the tabernacle. Everything about it was holy, providing powerful symbolic expression to the fact that God was not ordinary, nor could He be approached casually or be taken for granted. God wanted to meet with His people there but on His terms. Certainly, His glory was present and on display (Lev. 9:23), but Aaron's sons Nadab and Abihu were immediately consumed when they approached God inappropriately (Lev. 10:2). It was evident from their conduct with the golden calf that the Israelites were by no means worthy of dwelling with God or having His awesome presence among them. They did not obviously qualify for such a privilege, but God had chosen and called them into relationship with himself. They were now to be in covenant relationship with him, so the tabernacle served this second vital role. How could a people prone to sinning enjoy having a holy God in their midst? Sacrifice and atonement were vital and God himself provided the way forward.

An annual Day of Atonement was established in the Jewish calendar. First a bull was to be slain to atone for Aaron, the High Priest's sin, then two goats were to be presented before the Lord, one whose shed blood was to be sprinkled on the mercy seat to make atonement in the holy place. Then Aaron's hands were to be laid on the head of the live scapegoat, together with the confession of the sins of Israel and to be sent away into the wilderness. Guilt and uncleanness had to be removed from the people in order for God's presence to remain.

Here are glorious parallels for us, his end time church. We also celebrate atonement through the shedding of blood. These were God's people and He ordained the basis on which He would relate to them and deal with what defiled them. It was not for them to propose the grounds on which they could be in His presence. The pattern of the tabernacle came down from heaven. Moses had to copy what God showed him, including the mercy seat where blood was to be shed. God established a clear basis for atonement for their sins that satisfied His holiness. If God, who alone knew the value of sacrificial blood being shed, was at peace with them through that blood, they could be at peace with Him and with one another.

In Paul's wonderful letter to the Romans he establishes that, like Israel, we too have sinned and fallen short of the glory of God (Rom. 3:23), but then goes on to show that God has provided for us a propitiatory sacrifice in the blood of Christ, a mercy seat where atonement has been made for us. A substitute has taken our place and was punished on our behalf providing cleansing by means of his precious blood. As Peter puts it, 'You were not redeemed with perishable things like silver or gold… but with precious blood as of a lamb unblemished and spotless, the blood of Christ' (1 Pet. 1:19). What was to be done in the secrecy of the holiest place in the tabernacle was in the New Testament 'displayed publicly' on the Cross (Rom. 3:25). Justification through faith in the atoning death of Christ is now fundamental to God's church and it settles our relationship with God completely. God is satisfied, so, having been justified by faith, we have peace with God and access into this place of grace in which we stand (see Romans 5:1, 2).

The church at the end of the ages needs to be secure in the glorious truth of justification, otherwise we can tend to drift into the temptation of trying to justify ourselves. We have an enemy who is the accuser of the brothers (and sisters) who accuses us day and night, constantly trying to bring us into condemnation (Rev. 12:10). In response, you can be tempted to prove your worth or your righteousness by your own endeavour, unlike Paul who didn't seek a righteousness of his own derived from the law, but that which is through faith in Christ, the righteousness which comes from God on the basis of faith (Phil. 3:9).

No condemnation

Believers need to be secure that there is now no condemnation for those who are in Christ Jesus (Rom. 8:1). The blood of Christ has satisfied the heart of God. We reign in life, not through our own religious endeavour, but through receiving the abundance of grace and the free gift of righteousness (Rom. 5:17). Satan's snare is constantly to challenge us and move us from that secure position so that we are tempted to try to impress not only God, but ourselves and anyone else who might be watching by our sanctification. Justification through Christ's blood is our ground of appeal before God. It provides us with God-given peace. Sanctification must surely follow, but it is never our basis of peace with God.

Believers need to put on these truths like armour for the battle. God has provided a breastplate of righteousness to cover our hearts. We must simply receive it and put it on – the shield of faith must be taken up, the helmet of salvation put on. All these and other weaponry are freely supplied, but if forgotten or discarded we can become freshly vulnerable to every fiery dart that Satan hurls at us.

You have peace with God through Christ's atoning blood, not through religious endeavour. Never yield that ground. Never get lured into the quicksand of trying to justify yourself. Instead celebrate the mercy, grace and righteousness that Christ has purchased for you through his sacrifice. Wholeheartedly embrace what God has so freely given.

23

Come with us and we will do you good

The journey of God's people... Exodus 40:34–38,
Numbers 10:1–36

From now on the cloud dictated whether they moved or remained. It appeared over the tabernacle day and night, from evening to morning as a cloud of fire (Num. 9:15). Moses was instructed to hammer out two silver trumpets. At their command, the congregation were to gather and take up their positions anticipating God's protective hand upon them as they advanced. The time came for them to move for the first time from Sinai. The cloud lifted and they set out, no longer simply a crowd of former slaves, but in God-given formation on their way to the Promised Land. Judah led the way and the various tribes assembled in their appointed locations, embracing their various duties, including those who carried the Ark, with the tribe of Dan bringing up the rear.

As they marched in formation, they must have looked an impressive company, made awesome by the cloud of glory over them. With growing confidence, Moses chanted, 'Rise up O Lord! And let your enemies be scattered and let those who hate you flee before you.' When it came to rest, he said, 'Return O Lord to the myriad thousands of Israel' (Num. 10:35, 36). No longer the rabble that fled through the Red Sea, but a people beginning to take shape.

On their journey a fascinating conversation took place. Encountering his father-in-law, Moses invited him to join them. 'We are setting out to the place at which the Lord said, "I'll give it to you", come with us and we will do you good, for the Lord has promised good to Israel.' Surely a great invitation for the church to make her own, to shape both who we are becoming and who we are inviting along with us.

First, Moses made it clear that they were people on a journey. They were not static. The church's invitation should not be 'come to us', but rather 'come with us'. The church should not be regarded as a building at the end of a cul-de-sac, but a people on a highway. As pilgrims, we should invite people to join us on our mission. Becoming a static people should be anathema to us. The Jesus manifesto was, 'Go into all the world and preach the gospel to all creation' (Mark 16:15). The DNA of the church therefore is essentially a people on the move. The Father promised His Son the nations as His inheritance and the ends of the earth as His possession, and the church is His agent in accomplishing this in his name. The apostolic church was a sent church with Christ's words echoing in their hearts, 'As the Father sent me, so send I you' (John 20:21). Jesus commissioned his apostles to go and make disciples of all nations. Their response was instinctively to go and plant churches. This would be where disciples would be made in community, but the community must never forget that their *raison d'etre* is world evangelization.

The plan was never for churches to become static and introverted, but constantly to remember their essential calling. In the book of Acts, the Antioch church was founded by scattered believers from Jerusalem. Although they became a significant centre, they also formed a key sending base for the next push forward. Barnabas and Paul, key leaders in the church, were commissioned to go again on world mission.

Imagine someone being approached today with this invitation, 'Come with us and we will do you good.' He might want to ask a few questions such as 'Who are you? What makes you think that I might want to join you?' For the church to invite others to participate and identify with us, we need to be clear about who we are. Moses could have answered, 'We are all descendants from our great forefather Abraham.' God made him an extraordinary promise that through his descendants all the families of the earth would be blessed. God called him with a view to blessing the whole world. We are not simply a nomadic tribe, but his descendants, living with this promise of global significance.

So, the church must rediscover her global significance. Peter uncompromisingly proclaimed that, 'There is no other name given under heaven whereby men must be saved' (Acts 4:12). Internationally, the church is growing in an unprecedented way, predominantly in the southern hemisphere, but sadly not so much in the West where we need a rediscovery of our identity as a sent people.

Released slaves

Like Moses, we could actually testify that we were formerly slaves but we have experienced an amazing deliverance. We are essentially a people who has experienced an extraordinary salvation by God. We were not only saved from slavery; we were rescued from judgement through a lamb sacrificed on our behalf. Both slavery and judgement are behind us! We are a people freed by God! Not one of Egypt's army survived the Red Sea. Slavery is over. We would not be on this journey apart from our amazing deliverance.

We have also been called into an extraordinary relationship with the God who delivered us. When He set us free, He announced, 'Out of Egypt I called my Son.' Like Israel, we Christians are not only saved from slavery and peril, we have actually been adopted into God's family. He has become our father. You can join us. You can become part of the family. You can know God as father and join us in a unique personal relationship with God and His parental care. We are former slaves, but now sons.

I have another question. 'If I join you, where are you going?' That is also wonderful! We are going to a land, an inheritance which God has planned for us. For Israel, of course, a small territory known as Canaan, a strip of land at the eastern end of the Mediterranean where they would find cities that they had not built and vineyards that they had not planted, like a new creation waiting for them to inherit and populate, a land of blessing, milk and honey. For the church a greater destination awaits. 'Go into all the world and preach the gospel' is our commission. Our captain has been promised the nations as His inheritance and the ends of the earth as His possession and we are sent in His name. The church exists for this purpose, to bring the nations to Jesus.

Moses, even as he sang his mighty song of deliverance having crossed the Red Sea, was given prophetic insight. The exodus was not merely an escape for slaves who would scatter everywhere. God would 'bring them and plant them in the mountain of your inheritance, the place O Lord which you've made for your dwelling, the sanctuary O Lord which your hands have established' (Exod. 15:17). They were not only going to enter Canaan, but arrive at a particular mountain where a sanctuary for God's dwelling would be established. They would not always be a nomadic people. Inheritance awaited and a particular mountain would be selected to be called Zion, the joy of the whole earth. Jerusalem, which they would ultimately capture, where their king would be enthroned and where the temple would be built, would take on an awesome significance. Psalms would be written celebrating its stunning importance. It would be the place that God had specially chosen to dwell. Even as he crossed the Red Sea, Moses sang prophetically of the sanctuary that would be built there. Once again, in Solomon's day glory would fall, God's presence would flood the place. God's ultimate goal for these former slaves was a city with a temple, a people with God's presence at its heart.

All of this is, of course, translatable into Christian perspective. God's goal is still a people dwelling together in His presence. The beginning of the book of Acts demonstrates such a place where thousands were saved and were constantly together and overwhelmed by God's presence, a temple of living stones indwelt by the Holy Spirit. To be saved was to be added to a holy temple growing in the Lord (Eph. 2:21).

A place for me

One more question. What will happen to me if I join you? The answer was not, 'You can follow behind us all. Please try to keep up.' Rather, Moses said, 'You can be as eyes for us. You know where we should camp in the wilderness' (Num. 10:31). He was familiar with the territory. He would make a helpful contribution. Not that he would take over from the glory cloud to become their guide, but when the cloud stopped, he could bring helpful counsel regarding their camping site. Be 'eyes for us' has an extraordinary

New Testament ring, where we are told that the church is not only a temple for God's presence, but also a body with functioning members such as eyes, ears, hands and feet (1 Cor. 12:15–27). As members are added to the church, their gifts should be discerned, welcomed and developed. Disciples are not meant to simply be passive followers, but valued, functioning parts of a living body, all making their specific contribution. Realizing that you might have a role in the body of Christ can be a great discovery. Peter tells us, 'As each has received a special gift, we should employ it in serving one another as good stewards of the manifold grace of God' (1 Pet. 4:10). The purpose is not individualistic celebration of your particular gift, but the possibility of making a genuine contribution to the corporate life of a many-membered body.

Perhaps one last question. 'How come you are so confident? What grounds do you have for expecting success?' Moses' answer would be unequivocal, 'The Lord has promised good concerning Israel' (Num.10:29). We have God's word, His promise. Every step is a step towards what he has assured us of. The land is guaranteed. In the New Testament we read how Paul trembled at Corinth, but the Lord came to him in the night and said, 'Don't be afraid... I am with you... I have many people in this city' (Acts 18:10). The New Testament church advanced with the assurance of God's promised blessing and His personal commitment to their fruitfulness.

The church then, like Moses and the Israelites, is a people on the move, each local expression witnessing to its neighbourhood, while others will be released to advance the gospel to the ends of the earth and celebrate the truth that our common ancestor Abraham is indeed heir of the world (Rom. 4:13–16).

24

A leader under pressure

Leaders multiply... Numbers 11.

What a roller-coaster this journey was, particularly for Moses in his leadership role. Following the rather magnificent formation of the tribes, the covering glory cloud, Moses' triumphant shout 'Arise O Lord', the confident invitation to Moses' father-in-law to come with them, followed a particularly miserable chapter in his life.

The trouble started when the so-called 'rabble' began complaining (Num. 11:4). So, who were the rabble? They were probably what is called earlier 'the mixed multitude' who went with them from Egypt (Exod. 12:38). These may not have actually been Jewish people who fully comprehended the nation's unique identity and calling. Perhaps amazed at the plagues and their impact and also the growing reputation and esteem of Moses (Exod. 11:3) they simply added themselves to the released Jewish congregation. Now that circumstances looked negative, they were quick to lose their enthusiasm, somewhat reminiscent of the parable of the sower where Jesus spoke of seed scattered on the shallow soil, immediately responding to the word, but when the burning sun of opposition comes, they immediately fall away (Matt. 13:20–21).

Churches always face the possibility of having people in their ranks who are not necessarily captivated by God's purpose, but attach themselves to the community. Sadly, they can sometimes prove to have negative impact on those around them and a little leaven begins to spoil the lump (1 Cor. 5:6), so the Israelites began singing from their hymn sheet as well. 'Who will give us meat to eat?' Suddenly they were reminiscing and hallucinating about their former slave diet in Egypt, where they claimed they ate freely of cucumbers, melons, leeks, onion and garlic (Num. 11:5). By Numbers 16:13 they accuse Moses of bringing them out of a land 'flowing with milk and honey'. Distorted and selected memories fill their conversations and their complaints. The New Testament warns us that the tongue is a small member and how great a forest is set ablaze by it (James 3:5). Soon it seems like the whole congregation was weeping (Num. 11:10). God's anger was aroused by their ingratitude and resentment and Moses, caught and apparently squeezed between a disgruntled people and a God furious at their complaints, became the victim of more pressure than he could bear.

Leaders in any sphere inevitably carry more pressure than those who follow. This is particularly true in Christian leadership, seen modelled here in Moses' experience. He was gripped with a vision of the future, excited at the prospect of leading these former slaves into the Promised Land. The prospect of that future excited and motivated him as a leader. Leaders, focussed on the future, find it easier to cope with the short-term difficulties faced on the journey, whereas those following seem more aware of everyday challenges. The leader lives in an exciting future. Followers are often tempted to be more preoccupied with an incomplete present. Day to day burdens unsettle them while leaders can tend to take these problems in their stride, gaining energy from their anticipation of what lies ahead.

Moses' frustration boiled over and he challenged God, 'Why have you been so hard on your servant? Why have you laid the burden of this people upon me?' Getting increasingly wound up, he cried, 'Did I conceive all these people? Did I give them birth? Where am I to get meat to give all these people? The burden is too heavy for me. If you will treat me like this, kill me at once' (Num. 11:14–15). Moses became a leader with a death wish, similar to Elijah who prayed, 'Take my life from me' (1 Kings 19:4). The pressure on leaders can become claustrophobic. Two of the most famous figures in the Old Testament, both honoured by God to be present at the awesome Mount of Transfiguration, knew times when they would be happy to die to escape the pressure. Moses was effectively complaining to God that he was being asked to give more than he could provide. Many pastors have felt that challenge in endeavouring to fulfil their pastoral ministries. Trying to produce food for the flock, sermons for Sunday after Sunday following demanding weeks, they can face the devastating sense that, 'I simply can't do this anymore. Where am I supposed to get food for these people?' Overwhelmed by despair as they look at the challenge, they face their own sense of inadequacy. Nearly every pastor will have felt this pressure at some time. It might not reach the terrible depths of suicide that has rocked churches in recent years, but this weight of burnout can nevertheless be emotionally devastating and for many has led to abandoning pastoral ministry.

Is my hand shortened?

For Moses, the answer came in a fresh intervention from God whose question to Moses was simple yet profound. 'Is the Lord's power limited? His hand shortened?' (Num. 11:23). In all the pressure, Moses had allowed the problem to centre in his own ability to perform. He had actually failed to lean into God's awesome resources. At the Red Sea he had sung of the greatness of God's arm. Now, by implication, he was questioning whether God could solve the immediate pressing problem.

Every Christian has to answer the question of God's adequacy in the problems they face, but this is particularly true of leaders who often feel the intensity of the pressure and the challenge to provide answers. We all need to learn from Paul, where he spells out these tensions vividly. He tells the Corinthians of the excruciating pressures that he had faced in his recent apostolic role where he was burdened excessively, beyond strength, so that he despaired even of life, indeed had the sentence of death within himself, so that he would not trust in himself, but in God who raises the dead. The intensity he experienced was overwhelming, but he no longer looked within himself but to a God who raises people from apparent death (2 Cor. 1:8–9).

Despondency is a terrible enemy for those in leadership, but Paul learned a way through. He acknowledged the reality that we are not adequate in ourselves, but our adequacy comes from God who makes us adequate (2 Cor. 3:5–6). For some who take up Christian leadership, feeling strong and well-equipped, this discovery of complete inadequacy can come as a devastating shock. Others who knew their insufficiency before they started can be less overwhelmed, but nevertheless feel the intensity of pressure to perform. Paul's way through was to acknowledge that we have this treasure in very ordinary earthen vessels. The power, therefore, comes from God and not from us. He testified to being afflicted in every way, nevertheless not crushed, perplexed but not despairing, persecuted but not forsaken, struck down but not destroyed (2 Cor. 4:7–9). It can be comforting to know that these great heroes endured such pressure. Both Moses and Paul testify to heartbreaking pressure, yet ultimately they are servants. Ultimately it was not their battle. They were only in the conflict because God had put them there. Essentially, they were not really volunteers, but men whom God had apprehended and commissioned. Having called and sent them, God would not abandon them, but they needed fresh encounters with their Master who freshly empowered them.

His grace will always be enough if we refuse to see the problem as being centred in us and our personal resources, but remind ourselves that our adequacy is from God who makes us adequate.

25

Multiplied anointed leadership

Finding your seventy... Numbers 10:16–30

Loneliness and isolation had undoubtedly magnified the intensity of Moses' sense of inadequacy and pressure to perform in his leadership role. God had more to say to him regarding his desperate mood of despondency. In addition to reminding Moses of the great strength of His mighty arm, He compassionately gave instructions for the appointment of seventy more gifted leaders to stand with him.

First, we note that the seventy were to be gathered to God. Although Moses was to gather men known as elders in the nation, men who had presumably carried some responsibility in their various tribes and would have been recognized as such by the people, nevertheless they were to be brought to the Tent of Meeting. This was to be no mere human adjustment or administrative reshuffle of the troops. Their commissioning was to take place at the God-appointed Tent of Meeting where God's presence was specifically localized.

Although they had been already recognized and perhaps recommended by the people, it was important to understand that they were now to be specifically God-appointed and accountable to Him, not simply chosen by their tribes and answerable to them. They were to stand in God's presence, not simply stand before men. This was always the mark of true servants of God, exemplified by

Elijah when he confronted Ahab. His authority was based on his claim to stand before God (1 Kings 17:1). Authentic leadership does not simply reflect the wishes of the people they serve. Their authority is rooted in their awareness that they are accountable to the God who commissioned them. These men were to be seen as God-appointed and the Israelites needed to understand this. They were a unique nation under God and leadership appointment was not something casually handled or simply elected by the congregation. Human popularity was not the foundation of their office, but God's specific involvement. Popularity can come and go as Moses well knew, but God's authorization established true leadership. Israel was not a democracy. It had no elections.

In God's immediate presence, a particular transition took place. God came down in the cloud and took of the Spirit that was upon Moses, which had empowered and inspired him and placed him on the seventy elders and they prophesied. There was an immediate demonstration of God's manifest presence in each life. This was clearly no mere human selection and appointment, but God made it evident to all that He was personally involved. These were now God's appointed and equipped men.

This episode is somewhat reminiscent of Elisha's experience when he discerned his calling to be Elijah's replacement. Overwhelmed with the daunting awareness that he had to follow Elijah's awesome ministry, Elisha pleaded for a supply, even 'A double portion of your spirit to be upon me' (2 Cor. 2:9). Soon it would be observed by onlookers that the spirit of Elijah rests on Elisha (2 Kings 2:15). Although their cry was not 'the Spirit of God rests on Elijah', in both of these cases we must surely understand that this was a bestowal of the Holy Spirit, though the actual reference is to the spirit particularly associated with Moses and

Elijah. Elisha actually cried 'Where is the Lord, the God of Elijah?' (2 Kings 2:14).

Equipped by the spirit

The empowering of the seventy, the taking of the spirit who rested on Moses to now equip the seventy, rings an obvious New Testament bell as one is reminded of the Apostles being instructed by Jesus not to begin their ministries before they received power from on high (Luke 24:49). Like Elisha, they would no doubt be daunted at the responsibility of taking over the ministry that Jesus had initiated. In obedience they waited until they received. Once clothed with the Spirit of Christ, it became evident when people observed their boldness that they had been with Jesus (Acts 4:13). It was evident that the same power that rested on Christ was now enabling them. Jesus had promised that the one who fortifies would come and he had come and clothed them with the power needed for the task.

Later, Joshua would be clearly seen as Moses' successor and God instructed Moses to lay hands on him that the Spirit of wisdom might fill him (Deut. 34:9) for the task that he would fulfil, but this would come later in the narrative.

At this current stage in the story, Joshua was still being mentored by Moses and right here we are allowed to eavesdrop on some hands-on mentoring. When the seventy were invited to be present at the Tent of Meeting to receive the empowering Spirit it seems that two of those nominated, Eldad and Medad, were late on parade. We are not told why, but they simply remained in the camp. The Spirit nevertheless rested upon them and they prophesied as the others did. This caused quite a stir and a young man ran and told Moses. Joshua, who had served Moses from his youth, was enraged. How dare they? 'Moses, restrain them.' This was going to be an important discipling day for Joshua. Every reference to Joshua prior to the book of his name sheds light on the preparation he received for the role he would subsequently play.

The temptation to idolize those we love and respect can become very great. Honouring our leaders is an excellent trait, indeed a biblical command, but the danger can creep in that we take things too far. As is often the case the leader, Moses himself, was completely secure, untroubled and more than generous, but his close lieutenant leapt to his defence and endeavoured to squash any supposed rivalry. As it happens there was no sign of bad attitude in Eldad and Medad. Their only failure was being late to the gathering.

Sometimes those near to a leader can fail to represent him well and become jealous for his prestigious and unique position. They are, of course, involved since they are often close to that leader and may be hoping to sit on his right or left hand as his position of significance becomes ever greater. James and John showed similar ambition, but they, like Joshua, were still being trained. They not only had ambition to sit on the right hand and left hand of Jesus, but wanted to call down fire on those in Samaria who did not show them the proper respect (Luke 9:54). Jesus quickly corrected them. They did not yet understand his style or reflect his gentle character.

Moses responded with complete peace and poise, and also respect for the Holy Spirit who, like the wind, blows where he wills and refuses to be predictable or to bow to our neat and tidy expectations. Leaders do well to make room for Him and honour Him when he moves outside of their conceived expectations.

Joshua learned that day that Moses did not need his protection.

He was not only untroubled by Eldad and Medad's prophesying, like the Apostle Paul, he longed for the day when all of the Lord's people were prophets (Numbers 11:29; 1 Cor. 14:5). Leaders, secure in their own calling, are a great strength to the people of God, whereas the insecure can reproduce a culture of rivalry, suspicion and inappropriate defensiveness. Leaders can become afraid to show vulnerability, aiming to demonstrate an all-sufficiency that inspires an inappropriate respect or even a superiority. A leader aware of his calling and of God's hand upon him is able to reveal personal weakness. Such men can build teams who feel wanted, needed and honoured, not simply groups of clones simply idolizing and imitating their master.

Moses was delighted to discover men with their own experience of the Holy Spirit. They did not provide a threat but were a blessing. A similar characteristic can be found in David when mighty and extraordinarily gifted men came to him at Ziklag. He was not threatened by their evident gifts, but received them and made them captains so that what developed was called 'a great army, like the army of God' (1 Chronicles 12:18–22). Though David was a mighty and gifted leader, he was not a one-man-band with a growing army of fans and admirers. He was able to inspire and lead many who were themselves gifted. Moses was delighted to have in his ranks men who had their own experience of the Holy Spirit. Joshua was mentored by a secure leader.

26

Family conflict

Honour God. Numbers 12

Opposition from obvious enemies like the Amalekite army is one thing, but when those near and dear to you turn on you that is something else. Our next chapter reveals painful jealousy right in the midst of the camp. Not only in the camp, but from within Moses' family itself. His older brother and sister turned on him. His sister Miriam and brother Aaron, suddenly eaten up with envy and jealousy regarding his role and outrage that during his time away from Israel he had married a Kushite woman, spoke against him.

Once again Moses demonstrated extraordinary humility and freedom from self-importance, and it is in this context that scripture describes him as the humblest man on the face of the earth (Num. 12:3). God, however, would not stand idly by. He summoned Moses, Miriam and Aaron to the Tent of Meeting. Thoroughly exonerating Moses in his unique relationship with God, he expressed shock that they had found such freedom in dismissively speaking ill of him. No one else had ever been given such privileged access to God's presence. He was no self-appointed leader. God had chosen and called him for face-to-face fellowship. To speak against him was in some measure to fail to see God's activity and involvement in inviting him into his exclusive privileges. To challenge the servant was in some measure to challenge the master who had appointed him. Sometimes we are surprised by God's interventions. Moses was unperturbed, but God wasn't and nor was he going to simply watch from the sidelines. It seems to us maybe like a swift summons to the headmaster's office! My mind goes to the shock when God struck down Uzzah for putting his hand to the ark when it began to slip from the cart, or when Ananias and Sapphira fell dead in the days of the early church. There are moments when it becomes all too obvious that the scriptures are not mere human stories, myth invented by religious mystics, stamped by pedestrian morality or predictable story lines. From time to time, God himself appears with such shocking impact that to fear Him does not seem merely a religious duty, but plain common sense! He is frighteningly awesome.

Easy complaints about God's servants often come from people who have little fear of God or awareness of his jealous commitment to those He calls. They fail to grasp the wonder of the people of God and those specifically called by Him to serve them. They regard the people of God and their leadership with professional contempt. From time to time God himself steps in. Saul of Tarsus, secure in his own religious pedigree and dismissive of Jesus of Nazareth and his followers, had the shock of his life when God suddenly apprehended him. Falling to the ground, blind and thoroughly undone his whole world collapsed when God confronted him. He needed to be thoroughly reconstructed.

Whereas Miriam and Aaron found it a simple thing to oppose and challenge Moses, David, the man after God's own heart, showed a completely different perspective. Unjustly hounded by the profoundly backslidden King Saul, David had opportunity to kill him. Finding him asleep in a cave and at his mercy, and urged by his colleagues to kill him, David was mortified and shocked.

He was not going to raise his hand against the Lord's anointed. Having even cut off a small part of Saul's garment rather than raise his sword against the man himself, David was later conscience-stricken that he had taken even that step (1 Sam. 24:5).

Honour leadership

Honouring God's leadership is actually to honour God, especially when we realize that the people being led are God's chosen and beloved people, and when leadership is taken seriously and elders appointed with prayer and fasting and serious seeking of God, as in the New Testament (Acts 14:23). Sadly, the church in the twenty-first century is seen more as a democratic community. The attitude to leadership can be, 'We set them up, we take them down. Ultimately they answer to us.' This stands in stark contrast to the scripture which tells us to appreciate those who diligently labour among us and have the charge over us in the Lord and give us instruction, and to esteem them very highly in love (1 Thess. 5:12–13). Again, we are told 'obey your leaders and submit to them for they keep watch over your souls as those who will give an account' (Heb. 13:17). Meanwhile, the elders themselves are instructed to shepherd the flock of God, not lording it over those allotted to their charge, but proving examples, and finally accountable to the chief shepherd when he appears (see 1 Pet. 5:1–3). These elders are always referred to as plural rather than one isolated figure. As a team they should work out their mutual accountability and respect for one another in a context of reverence and awareness of their privileges.

When the cloud had withdrawn from over the tent, Miriam was found to be leprous, as white as snow. Once again Moses stepped into his familiar role as mediator and intercessor, pleading with God to heal her. God's ultimate reply was healing and full reinstatement, but seven days must first elapse. She was shut outside the camp and the people did not move until she was received again. The whole nation was taught the seriousness of the offence so that all were affected.

When gross sin was uncovered in the Corinthian church Paul's great concern was that they had not mourned or felt any corporate responsibility. The one who had done the deed should have been removed. Paul warned that a little leaven could leaven the whole lump. Action should be taken (1 Cor. 5:1–13). In his later letter he urged them to forgive and comfort and reaffirm their love to the guilty one. The punishment had been sufficient (2 Cor. 2:6–7). So, with Miriam. Sufficient punishment had been experienced. Full restoration to the people who could move on together. God's anger had been aroused but, as ever, his mercy endures forever.

27

The unbelieving spies

What do you see? Numbers 13, 14

I wonder if you have heard of Shaphat, son of Hori, or Igal, son of Joseph? I think it unlikely, but for a short time they must have been national heroes. No doubt their wives were proud of them and their children celebrated their fame. Why? Because from their whole tribes numbering several thousands these leading men were uniquely chosen. They were to represent their tribe for a noble task, namely to go and spy out the land of Canaan. The reason they are not famous is that the Bible celebrates men and women of faith, but these were two of the ten who brought back a report of unbelief. Their names, though all listed as selected men, were quickly forgotten (Num. 13:5–15).

Our story has reached a crucial yet tragic moment in Israel's history. They had reached the borders of the land that God had promised. Moses instructed the twelve to spy out the land. Are the people strong or weak? Few or many? Is the land good or bad, cities open or fortified? And bring back some of the fruit! They entered and returned carrying luscious grapes, pomegranates and figs, but more significantly they returned with a jaundiced view. From their perspective the task of taking the land was impossible. There were giants there. We became like grasshoppers in our own sight and so we were in theirs, was their considered opinion. The majority voice of doom and despair prevailed. The voices of Joshua and

Caleb were refused and ignored. They alone were confident that with God's hand upon them they would prevail. They were assured that with God's promised help the Canaanites would be their prey.

This represented one of the tragic days of Israel's history, and one that is remembered as a profound failure due to seemingly reasonable unbelief. God had promised them the land, but when they looked at the challenge faced, they didn't find corresponding faith to overcome. Only Joshua and Caleb saw clearly, but they were outnumbered, their voices ignored. News quickly spread through the camp and, once again, Moses and Aaron bore the brunt of their anger and dismay. The hostility even developed to the point when they were ready to appoint another leader who could take them back to Egypt. Fear ran rampant among them. What would happen to their wives and children? They would become plunder for their enemies.

We are given a brief account of the conflict between faith and fear. Joshua and Caleb were bubbling over with confidence that with God's help they could enter the stunning land that lay before them and which He had promised to give them, while the other ten were paralysed with fear. Faith and fear are always enemies fighting for our hearts and minds. No wonder Jesus said frequently, don't fear, only believe. You simply cannot do both at once. With that in mind, it is so important that we understand that faith is not simply optimism. It is not something inherent in certain personalities, but absent in others who have a more negative view of life. It is not simply that some see the glass half full and some see it half empty. Joshua and Caleb were not just a couple of upbeat guys who look on the bright side

Their faith was based on something far more substantial. They understood that to turn back was actually to 'rebel against the Lord'

(Num. 14:9). Moses had not sent the spies in so that they could assess whether it was viable to take the land, but simply to report the situation there. The reason they had arrived at Canaan was that God had led them there intending them to take it. Tragically their human unbelieving perspective intervened and actually prevailed. Considering their own limitations, they concluded that they were not able to enjoy success in battle. The give-away line is found in their testimony, 'We became like grasshoppers in our own sight and so were we in their sight' (Num. 13:33). They may have regarded this as a plain fact. One could imagine their cry, 'Let's simply face the facts!'

It's personal with God

They may have been shocked by God's response, 'How long will these people despise me?' (Num. 14:11). I think they might have bleated that they were not despising God, but simply facing the facts. The enemy was strong and entrenched and in fortified cities. Let's face it! God, however, saw it as a personal afront to him, which Joshua and Caleb had understood, but the other spies had not. Our two heroes comprehended that faith had an object, namely the all-powerful covenant-keeping God. It was a matter not of optimism, but of confidence in God. Faith is actually personal and relational and demonstrates that the believer has confidence in the one who has made the promises. It is fundamental that the church, pursuing its God-appointed role to bring the gospel to every nation, advances with that awareness.

As children of Abraham we should emulate his superb example. Having been promised by God that he would become the father of many nations we are told that he did not weaken in faith when he considered his own body, which was as good as dead, since he was about 100 years old, or when he considered the barrenness of Sarah's womb. No unbelief made him waiver concerning the promise of God, but he grew strong in his faith as he gave glory to God, fully convinced that God was able to do what he had promised (Rom. 4:19–21). God promises what He is able to perform. Faith finds its resting place there and finds boldness to press forward into the works that He has prepared beforehand for us to walk in. They looked at the situation and assessed it from a natural perspective, weighing up their apparent weakness and the enemy's evident strength. God, on the other hand, regarded it as a matter of personal afront. 'How long will these people despise me?' (Num. 14:11). We shall find it helpful to understand that faith for the Christian is a personal and living issue based on a relationship. The more we get to know our God, the more inclined we shall be to trust him. The greater we see Him to be, the smaller will be the problems that we face.

As Joshua and Caleb stood their ground pleading for confidence in God, the congregation's mood grew even uglier, planning to stone them and silence their voice. Then the glory of the Lord appeared to all the sons of Israel. He spoke and what He said was terrifying. He was ready to completely disinherit them, cut them off and destroy them with pestilence (Num. 14:12). Again, the offer came to Moses that God would make a fresh start with him, starting a new nation through his family. Once again, our intrepid hero, the magnificent mediator/intercessor Moses, stood his ground, pleading that God's glory and fame itself was at stake, the heathen will mock that the Lord was not able to bring them into the land He promised them.

His argued intercession was magnificent. With no personal

ambition to become the new Abraham fathering his own nation, instead his preoccupation was entirely the reputation of his God. His final argument was awesome. He had earlier longed for a revelation of God's glory and the Lord had passed in front of him and proclaimed, 'The Lord, the Lord God, compassionate and gracious, slow to anger and abounding in loving kindness and truth, who keeps loving kindness for thousands, who forgives iniquity transgression and sin' (Exod. 34:6, 7). Moses had had a profound glimpse into the very heart of God. Now he argued from this superb self-revelation of God's character. Moses really did know God and his expectation was shaped by that knowledge. He pleaded for the people to be pardoned according to the greatness of God's loving kindness. God's response was immediate, 'I have pardoned according to your word.'

What followed was unexpected and magnificent. God did not say, 'As I live you shall possess Canaan', but instead proclaimed, 'As I live all the earth will be filled with the glory of the Lord' (Num. 14:21). Possessing Canaan was evidently a simple stepping stone to God's great goal to fill the whole earth with His glory. Taking Canaan was simply one of the chapters leading to the ultimate conclusion.

As our story ends, we see Shaphat and Igal, whose names introduced our chapter, together with the other eight unbelieving spies, died in plague before the Lord, but Joshua and Caleb remained alive. They lived by faith! Later, when Joshua came to the land, we hear that, rather than seeing the Israelites as grasshoppers as the spies had feared, the Canaanites had been terrified and were still terrified forty years later. They had heard about the crossing of the Red Sea and their hearts had melted away and no courage remained, 'For the Lord your God He is God of heaven above and earth beneath' (Josh. 2:10,11). How wrong the unbelieving spies were. How distorted their view.

Let's learn to fight the good fight of faith. It is a fight worth fighting. Yes, sometimes we are aware of our own frailty and we can tremble, but if we keep looking to our faithful and powerful God, we will prove Him faithful and magnify His name in His onward journey to fill the nations with His glory.

28

Korah's rebellion

Prayer is revolutionary. Numbers 16

As we pursue the story of the Israelites through the wilderness, Moses emerges as an increasingly towering figure, faithful, stable, compassionate and utterly centred in God's glory and purpose. It's fascinating to see how his role is regarded by scripture. Paul says, 'They were all baptised into Moses in the sea and in the cloud' (1 Cor. 10:2). An extraordinary statement. Hosea adds, 'By a prophet the Lord brought Israel from Egypt and by a prophet he was kept' (Hosea 12:13). From God's perspective he was fundamental to their success. Throughout their journey, their very existence depended on Moses' intercession, his walk with God and obedience to God's every command. Twice God offered him the opportunity to be the head of the new nation, which he rejected out of his devotion to God's reputation and glory and out of his compassion for the nation. God himself boasted, 'My servant Moses, he is faithful in all my household, with him I speak mouth to mouth' (Num. 12:7–8).

Against this background of a man in a unique relationship with God comes the next major event in our story. A rebellion headed by Korah, a Levite, together with 250 leaders of the congregation, confronted Moses with the claim that the whole congregation was holy and that the Lord was among them all. To this he added the accusation that Moses, together with Aaron, had exalted themselves above the assembly. At this we are told that Moses fell on his face (Num. 16:4). We must understand this was not out of personal afront, but because he knew how offensive this was to the God who had called and commissioned him. Their lack of respect for Moses was in effect a lack of reverence for God, a total insensitivity to the unique role that Moses fulfilled entirely at God's instigation. Although he was, as God had described him, the meekest man on earth, he was not unaware of his own unparalleled calling.

Like a bull in a china shop, Korah had barged into forbidden territory with crass ignorance and arrogance. The outcome would become one of the most dramatic displays of God's power in the whole narrative. Moses acted swiftly and decisively, instinctively knowing that this was time not for debate or discussion, but for clarity and that of a dramatic nature. These were men of renown, Levites already separate from the rest of the congregation with privileged duties of service at the Tabernacle. Their extraordinary contempt for Moses was matched by that of Dathan and Abiram, two of their co-conspirators, who refused Moses' summons and hurled further abuse, accusing Moses of 'lording it over them' (Num. 16:13).

As the glory cloud of the Lord's presence returned, although Moses was the one sinned against, he once again fulfilled the role of mediator. God's own fury at this rebellion in the camp led to His declared purpose to consume the whole congregation. Moses was on his face before God pleading for the people. Again, his intercession prevailed.

God required the guilty men to be separated from the rest of the camp. In opposing Moses, they had despised the Lord (Num. 16:30). Moses asked that they should be dealt with very specifically so that it was manifestly clear that God himself was expressing His judgement. Moses even asked that their death should be unlike the common fate of any man. He asked that the ground open and swallow them! Immediately after Moses' thought was expressed, the ground literally opened and they were swallowed out of sight while fire from heaven consumed the remaining 250, a phenomenal display of God's power and displeasure.

In spite of this unprecedented display of divine intervention the people, now apparently entrenched in aggressive hostility, grumbled further against Moses and Aaron, accusing them of causing the death of the Lord's people (Num. 16:41). Once again, the glory cloud appeared and Moses was told to stand aside so that God could instantly consume the whole congregation. As before, Moses was on his face, pleading for the people while Aaron ran into the midst of the congregation where the plague of judgement was rapidly advancing and, standing between the dead and the living, made atonement and the plague was checked.

God's endorsement

One would expect that no further proof was needed to establish Moses' and Aaron's credentials for leadership, but sadly rivalry and competitiveness was still lurking. God directed that a dramatic demonstration of Aaron's calling should be arranged with a view to ending the grumbling of the rebels. Twelve rods were to be volunteered from the respective tribes, each with the appropriate name written on it. They should all be deposited in the Tent of Meeting. On the following day, Aaron's rod alone bore buds, blossom and ripe almonds. The other eleven remained dry and fruitless rods. The exercise was intended to end the grumbling which they had embraced as a way of life.

The pattern of resisting leaders whom God has chosen frequently raises its head in scripture and it always represents at root rebellion against God. Nehemiah's heart was broken when he heard of Jerusalem's walls being broken down and its gates burned. He wept, fasted and prayed for days. God apprehended and sent him to rebuild his beloved city. On arrival, he met with life-threatening hostility, mockery, questioning of motives and outright accusation that he was planning to be king. David, anointed but faithfully serving Saul, was falsely accused of inappropriate ambition and was hounded relentlessly. The Apostle Paul was frequently ridiculed and opposed by those hostile to him and his calling, and of course attempts to ridicule and oppose Jesus, the upstart carpenter's son, were almost a daily occurrence, shared also by his followers, those unlearned fishermen from Galilee!

These all, sent by God to be saviours and deliverers, were greeted with hostility. Deeply rooted in the human condition is a refusal to embrace God's rule. Sadly, even among God's people that rebellion can still surface, but embarrassed and fearful to outrightly oppose God, they express their subterfuge towards God's servants. So tragic when these human traits find their way into God's church where leadership should be loved, honoured and respected as God's gracious gift to His people! Jesus ascended on high and in love gave gifts to his body to strengthen and encourage. These gifts should be received with gratitude and appreciation. Paul's request is that we appreciate those who diligently labour amongst us and have the charge over us in the Lord and give us instruction, and that we esteem them very highly in love because of their work (1 Thess. 5:12–13).

Tragically, the Israelites were continually characterized by murmuring and complaining, particularly against their leaders. They had become a generation in unbelief, having turned back at Canaan's threshold. Failure to walk in faith devastated any sense of purpose and quickly led to multiplied expressions of murmuring. The anticipation of better days and of inheriting the land had been lost. Now they merely endured existence. A mood of dissatisfaction and despondency dominated them. Such a mood often predominates modern society. Believers are called upon not to get sucked into the prevailing culture, but, indwelt by God's Spirit and with God's promises leading us forward, to demonstrate that we have a different citizenship, speaking a different language and celebrating a different hope profoundly grateful for the leaders that God has provided.

Korah's rebellion provides a shocking reminder to God's perspective on careless and presumptuous attitudes. May God help us to have a sensitivity which seems thoroughly absent in this story.

29

Balaam's blessing

God speaks through a donkey. Numbers 23–24

Against the backdrop of Israel's repeated acts of rebellion and
Moses' faithful leadership comes a story which, in some ways,
could be regarded as almost comic yet shows with great clarity
and tenderness God's magnificent attitude to His chosen people.
Israel had begun to enjoy some military success as they once
again drew near to Canaan. Battles had been fought and won. In
dread and fear of the advancing hoard, Moab's King Balak sent
for an extraordinary figure named Balaam, one who appeared to
be gifted with formidable prophetic authority. He was prepared
to pay the man with divination fees to curse Israel on his behalf.
However, the renegade prophet received a harsh warning, first
from God directly and subsequently from the lips of no less
than his own donkey, providing a shocking reprimand. He was
forbidden to curse Israel. However, Balak was determined to buy
his man, confident in his power to cast a spell on his enemies.
Although Balaam was paid his divination fee, what follows was no
curse, but some of the most lyrical words describing God's view of
Israel and His unbreakable commitment to them.

Balaam began his incantation by asking, 'How can I curse whom
God has not cursed?' and proceeded with a glowing description of
Israel as a unique nation dwelling apart. Shocked and dismayed
that Balaam had blessed and not cursed Israel, Balak urged him to

133

take a stance from a different viewpoint, maybe more favourable territory on high ground, and to try again. Balaam's second word was even more striking. He began with a glorious and dramatic statement of God's integrity:

> "God is not a man, that he should lie,
> Nor a son of man, that he should repent;
> Has he said, and will he not do it?
> Or has he spoken, and will he not make it good?
> Behold, I have received commandment to bless;
> When he has blessed then I cannot revoke it."
>
> (Num. 23:19–20)

He then added that God had not observed misfortune in Jacob nor seen trouble in Israel. How can this be? Trouble was writ large all over them. They were full of mischief and rebellion. How come this amazingly positive utterance? Surely because by virtue of God's provision of The Tabernacle with the accompanying mercy seat and annual Day of Atonement, God saw them from a completely different perspective. Sin had been atoned for. Blood had been shed for the nation's failures. God had received their sacrifices and regarded their sin as covered.

Balaam continued:

> "The Lord his God is with him,
> And the shout of a king is among them.
> God brings them out of Egypt,
> He is for them like the horns of the wild ox.
> For there is no omen against Jacob,
> Nor is there any divination against Israel.

> Behold, a people rises like a lioness,
> And as a lion it lifts itself;
> It will not lie down until it devours the prey,
> And drinks the blood of the slain."
>
> (Num. 23:21b–24)

Horrified, Balak interjected, 'Don't curse them at all or bless them at all,' and thought he would try yet once more in another location on even higher ground, the top of Mount Peor. Altars were constructed, bulls and rams prepared and offered. Extraordinary religious syncretism was on display, but neither God nor Balaam could be bribed. The Spirit of God came upon him:

> "How fair are your tents, O Jacob,
> Your dwellings, O Israel!
> Like valleys that stretch out,
> Like gardens beside the river,
> Like aloes planted by the Lord,
> Like cedars beside the waters…"
>
> (Num. 24:5–6)

Further poetic language rose to a further crescendo:

> "God brings him out of Egypt,
> He is for him like the horns of a wild ox.
> He will devour the nations who are his adversaries,
> And will crush their bones in pieces,
> And shatter them with His arrows.
> He crouches, he lies down as a lion,
> And as a lion, who dares rouse him?

135

Blessed is everyone who blesses you,
And cursed is everyone who curses you."

(Num. 24:8–9)

In these sublime poetic prophecies, God revealed His unique commitment to His people. In spite of their repeated failures, He declared himself avowed to them in covenant love. He was for them. He was among them. He would fight their battles and crush their enemies. They would inevitably enjoy success. The man hired to curse them could only find himself blessing them, because God is not a man that He should lie. He had blessed and it could not be reversed.

There is so much here for the church at the end of the ages to note. First, when God makes a promise, He will not reverse it. There may be setbacks, heartbreaks and even judgements handed out on unbelieving, rebellious generations, such as those who defied God when the ten spies returned with their negative, God-dismissing report. Yet as God said at that very time, 'As surely as I live,' (and what follows that kind of introduction will most certainly take place!) 'all the earth will be filled with the glory of the Lord'. The rebellion at Kadesh Barnea delayed their advance by a whole generation, but God's purpose kept marching on. The unbelieving fathers died in the wilderness, yet their sons would go on and inherit the land. This 'taking' of the land, however, will only be because Yahweh has given it to them and fought for them.

Like Israel, the church may go through seasons of unbelief and even generations when the Bible would be hidden, but God will always raise up His Luthers and Tyndales, His Whitefields and Wesleys, and His purposes will advance again. As Balaam pronounced, 'God is not a man that He should lie.' From the beginning He promised Abraham that in his seed, all the families of the earth would be blessed.

God's attitude to His people is revealed here. He is not ignorant of our weaknesses and failures, and will punish unbelief. Seeing them walking in the provision of atonement and mercy, God would stay true to them because ultimately their guilt had been covered. Now He will be for His church, 'Like the horns of a wild ox'. He will prevail in them and through them. As Paul triumphantly cried, 'If God is for us, who is against us? Who will bring a charge against God's elect?' (Rom. 8:31–33). 'The accuser of our brothers has been thrown down' (Rev. 12:10).

Ultimately a great multitude that no man can number will gather not as a scruffy shambles, but as a bride that has made herself ready, clothed in fine linen bright and clean, invited to the marriage supper of the Lamb, coming down out of heaven made ready as a bride for her husband, arrayed in a righteousness provided for her through the obedience of her Saviour. God's purpose for His people will ultimately prevail. They will be His people and He will be their God and He will dwell among them in a new earth and a new heaven.

Our story bears testimony to a people gradually transformed from a slave rabble into a disciplined army under Joshua. An army that kept silent for six days as they encircled Jericho in formation and, in obedience, shouted on day seven. Their triumph echoes down through the centuries, celebrated by the great shout, 'By faith the walls of Jericho fell down!' (Heb. 11:30).

30

Moses' task completed

Dead, but not forgotten... Deuteronomy 34

As the end drew near for Moses, we find him still awestruck at the wonder of God's majesty and arguing that God had surely *only begun* to show him His greatness. He was a truly God-besotted man. He also cried to God that he might enter the Promised Land. But the matter was settled. His role was fulfilled.

The rebel generation had died in the wilderness and the new generation was beginning to enjoy military victories that augured well for the conflict that lay ahead across Jordan. Sixty cities had been defeated (Deut. 3:4). Hopes were rising, a new day was about to dawn. The land was waiting for them. Yet Moses, their great captain, a giver of hope whose driven urgency, singular loyalty and remorseless energy had brought them this far, would no longer be leading them. At God's direction he had identified Joshua as his successor and laid hands on him before the people. God's programme was to advance and the next generation's leader was in place.

Undoubtedly, Moses' unique role and vision for the future had sustained the people thus far. Uniquely preoccupied with God's glory, he had repeatedly fought in prayer for their survival and success while they regularly showed short-sightedness and even a preoccupation with Egypt, regarding it with excessive and distorted nostalgia, frequently pleading to return there. It was on one occasion when once again their rebellious indiscipline had erupted and they had demanded water, that Moses without precedent spilled over with frustration and fury. Usually the epitome of patience and longsuffering, he lost it. Instead of simply speaking to the rock which would provide the water as God had commanded him, Moses struck it twice and harangued the people harshly, denouncing them as rebels. As Paul tells us, we have this treasure in earthen vessels, demonstrating that the surpassing greatness of the power is from God not us. On this occasion the earthen vessel was on display. Disobedient and angry, he lashed out and failed to fulfil his calling. God's judgement was swift and, although Moses was appropriately acquiescent at the time (Num. 20:12), he later pleaded with God to change His verdict, only to find God unyielding. He was invited to climb Mount Pisgah and gaze at the land, but to abandon the idea of going in (Deut. 3:27).

It could be said that he paid the ultimate price. He had been a genuine mediator, fully identifying with the people and pleading their cause, but also repeatedly standing before the people on God's behalf, reminding them of their covenant relationship with the Lord who had delivered them from slavery in Egypt. At the golden calf debacle, he shared God's anger and expressed his fury, smashing the tablets containing the Ten Commandments and forcing the people to reduce the calf to dust, mingle it with water and drink it. Yet on other occasions he pleaded with God that He would show mercy, even offering to have his own name removed from God's book that the nation might live. God had dismissed that request, but his identification with the people ultimately resulted in his not entering in. No other biblical figure fulfilled such a role as a mediator and so provided a type of Christ willing to spend his life that others might live. Moses beautifully foreshadowed the oneness with the Father and his identification with his followers that took Jesus to the cross.

Moses had been an awesome prophet. He declared God's ultimate goal in his stunning prophetic song at the Red Sea. He would complete his role once again in prophetic mode with his final prophecy. Among many other things, he sang of God being like a mother eagle carrying them in his purpose, yet again spoke of their unfaithfulness and finally prophesied over each individual tribe. He concluded with the ultimate truth, 'Blessed are you O Israel. Who is like you? A people saved by the Lord' (Exod. 33:20). That fundamental truth summed up their identity. God had set his love upon them, selecting them for the unfathomable and impenetrable reason that He loved them (Deut. 7:7–8). He had chosen them to be a people for His own possession out of all the peoples on the face of the earth. Moses had been the mediator, the lightning rod, communicating the burning fire of God's jealous zeal for such an unworthy people. Their success so far seemed inseparably bound up with Him. Truly they had been baptized into Moses in the cloud and in the sea (1 Cor. 10:2).

The law's limitations

In the final analysis, he was a mere man with human limitations. Moses could not take them into their Promised Land, as also the New Testament makes it clear that the law could not bring us into our promised inheritance. The law was inevitably limited, it's role temporary. Only Jesus (our Joshua) could bring us right in. Moses, representing the law, was not permitted to bring them in and so fulfilled that limited role.

As Paul would spell out in his letter to the Galatians, the law had a clearly defined and limited role. Only Jesus can transform us and bring us into full possession of all that was promised by the work of the Holy Spirit. Moses, the one identified with the law, was not permitted to enter, but Moses the man had served God with enormous fortitude, courage and devotion. As God's faithful servant he brought the people to the brink of the promised inheritance and led them with skilful hands.

Though baptized into Moses, they were essentially God's people. God had uniquely taken them for himself from within another nation by awesome signs and wonders by his mighty delivering hand. Loved and specially chosen, but led through the wilderness that he might humble them, testing them to discover their hearts and whether or not they would keep His commandments and wanting them to understand that man does not live by bread alone, but by every word proceeding from the mouth of God (Deut. 8:3). As a people, they can only be understood in the light of God's ultimate mission to all the nations. God so loved the world that he chose Israel.

Now we, the church, not the replacement for Israel but Israel internationalized and extended as was always God's purpose, are to live as a chosen race, a royal priesthood, a holy nation, a people for God's own possession so that we might proclaim the excellencies of Him who called us out of darkness into His marvellous light. Once we were not a people, but now we are the people of God, had not received mercy, but now have received mercy (see 1 Pet. 2:9–10). His treasured possession.

Our last glimpse of Moses is unexpectedly found in the New Testament, where Jesus took his three leading disciples to a mountain top and was stunningly transfigured before them. The glory of God flooded through him, not as a reflection as with

Moses, but shining out from deep within and not concealed by a veil, since his glory poured through his very clothes, which themselves, 'became as bright as a flash of lightning' (Luke 9:29). Once again the glory cloud appeared, but we might be fascinated to eavesdrop on the conversation taking place between Jesus, Moses and Elijah, who we are told 'appeared in glorious splendour'. They were discussing what was about to happen in Jerusalem where Jesus would soon be executed, but notice how they referred to it. Literally they spoke of the departure that he was going to accomplish there. Extraordinary to regard a death as an 'accomplishment'. Surely death is defeat! Yet light is shed when we discover that the word translated 'departure' in the original Greek is 'exodus'! Jesus was about to accomplish his exodus! He, by his death and resurrection, was going to release slaves not simply from Egypt, but purchase them for God with his blood from every tribe, tongue, people and nation and make them to be a kingdom of priests to God and they will reign on earth (see Rev. 5:9–10).

In his exodus Jesus has broken the bondage of slavery and released us into sonship and an eternal inheritance. As our Passover he was slaughtered, thoroughly atoning for our guilt and shame, but through his resurrection he has made a way into freedom and inheritance. Moses had been faithful in God's house as a servant. Yet Christ is faithful as a son over God's house. And we are his house if we hold on to our courage and the hope of which we boast (see Heb. 3:5–6).

May God help us in our pilgrimage following our shepherd leader, the one like Moses (Deut. 18:18), our utterly unique mediator, as he establishes His kingdom in every nation and 'leads many sons to glory' (Heb. 2:10).

Notes

1   An excellent account of prayer in the Old Testament can be found in Gary Millar's NSBT, *Calling on the Name of the Lord: A Biblical Theology of Prayer* (Apollos, London, 2016).

2   Chris Wrights' *Here Are Your Gods! Faithful Discipleship in Idolatrous Times* (IVP, London, 2020) and Tim Keller's *Counterfeit Gods* (Hodder & Stoughton, London, 2010) both unpack this.

3   If you want to read about this, more detail can be found in an article by Louis H. Feldman, *Josephus' Portrait of Moses: Part Two, The Jewish Quarterly Review*, Vol. 83, No. 1/2 (Jul.–Oct., 1992), pp. 7–50 (44 pages).

4   2020 saw the publication of two powerful, beautiful books that help us understand this. Dane Ortlund's *Gentle and Lowly: The Heart of Christ for Sinners and Sufferers* (Crossway, Wheaton, 2020) would make a fine devotional to help us see ourselves as Jesus does. Julian Hardyman's *Jesus, Lover of My Soul* (IVP, London, 2020) offers a powerful reading of the Song of Songs, which reminds us of the love Jesus has for us. *Jesus, Lover of My Soul* also has two profound chapters on pornography, which is often a sin we struggle to deal with.

5   J. I. Packer, *Knowing God*, Hodder, London, 1973, p. 88.

6   This is a modern worship song by Jeremy Camp, *You're Worthy of My Praise*. Lyrics can be found here: <https://www.azlyrics.com/lyrics/jeremycamp/youreworthyofmypraise.html> [accessed 23/10/20].

Further reading

I'd like to commend and recommend a few books that I have found helpful in thinking about the story of Moses, and some of the issues that have come up as we have followed his journey.

On Exodus

AW. Ross Blackburn, *The God Who Makes Himself Known: The Missionary Heart of the Book of Exodus* (Apollos, 2012)

Oren R. Martin, *Bound for the Promised Land: The Land Promise in God's Redemptive Plan* (Apollos, 2015)

James Robson, *Honey from the Rock: Deuteronomy for the People of God* (Apollos, 2013)

On Prayer

Don. A. Carson, *A Call to Spiritual Reformation: Priorities from Paul and His Prayers* (IVP, 2011)

Paul Miller, *A Praying Life: Connecting with God in a distracting world* (NavPress, 2017)

Andrew Murray, *The Ministry of Intercession* (Aneko, 2016)

On Leadership

Alexander Balmain Bruce, *The Training of the Twelve* (1871)

Paul David Tripp, *Dangerous Calling: The Unique Challenges of Pastoral Ministry* (IVP, 2012)

Bill Hull, *The Disciple-Making Pastor: Leading Others on the Journey of Faith* (Baker, 2007)

J. Robert Clinton, *The Making of a Leader* (NavPress, 2012)